Having Little, Being Much

Having Little, Being Much

A Chronicle of
Fredy Perlman's Fifty Years

by
Lorraine Perlman

Black & Red
Detroit
1989

Available from:
Black & Red
P.O. Box 02374
Detroit, Michigan 48202

CONTENTS

Introductory Note

Years before he articulated the dichotomy between being and having, Fredy consciously chose to have little. His aspiration to be much was initially expressed either in Faustian terms or using a humanist vocabulary which applauded the self-realization of the individual. Alert to ways in which conventional attitudes and institutional restrictions stifle the individual, Fredy saw himself in a social context and understood that his own self-realization was inseparable from that of his contemporaries. Even while railing against their acceptance of social fetters which gives life to repressive institutions, he had no ambition to be in a position to tell others what to do with *their* lives. A crucial part of his own vision for a meaningful life was that every individual have the opportunity to realize his or her creative potential.

With a view to changing institutions and the society in which he lived, Fredy devoted a good part of his fifty years to a study of philosophy, economics and history but his desire for change was incompatible with any theory which allowed that an authoritarian regime might be appropriate under certain circumstances or for certain populations. He sought to expose and discredit inhibiting institutions and hoped the collective efforts of his contemporaries would succeed in dismantling the institutions, thereby enlarging everyone's scope for self-realization.

In the days when we lived in a rooming house near Columbia University in New York City, Fredy used his own words—and spoke in the present tense—to express the sentiments that William Wordsworth put this way:

> I began
> To meditate with ardour on the rule
> And management of nations; what it is
> And ought to be; and strove to learn how far
> Their power or weakness, wealth or poverty,
> Their happiness or misery, depends
> Upon their laws, and fashion of the State.
>
> O pleasant exercise of hope and joy!
> For mighty were the auxiliars which then stood
> Upon our side, we who were strong in love!
> Bliss was it in that dawn to be alive,
> But to be young was very Heaven!

Fredy was too conscious of the recent suffering imposed on millions of human beings to aspire to "bliss" in the contemporary world, but, like the poet, felt that he and the "auxiliars" strong in love would be mighty enough to root out many of society's fetters. The challenge exhilarated him; his confidence was persuasive to me and to others.

Fredy did not consider generous sentiments toward fellow beings to be unusual; he attributed a comparable goodwill to his associates and assumed their commitment was equal to his. Though not prone to exaggerating his or other individuals' influence on world events, he nevertheless viewed a person's chosen activities in a large social context. He scrutinized his own choices closely, wanting them to be exemplary.

My original intent in writing this memoir was to trace Fredy's intellectual history, his changing views on self-realization. But the events of his life, his chosen activities and his friends had such an enormous influence on his views that I concentrated on biographical facts, convincing myself that this account would contribute to an understanding of Fredy's intellectual trajectory.

Fredy's life was not a tragic one. If he had acute disappointments in his 51 years, he did not articulate them; whereas he frequently professed satisfaction with his choices. He never expressed regret about our decision not to have children nor was he envious of successful professionals, either of their activity, possessions or prestige. Fredy liked the role of social critic and saw himself as part of a long and admirable tradition. Since he never admitted the possibility of a society that would not need criticism, he hoped his insights would contribute to the efforts of other dissidents.

The frequent references I make to Fredy's essays and novels may seem fragmentary to individuals who have not read his works. In general, I have assumed that the reader is familiar with much of Fredy's writing and I have not attempted to analyze or describe texts that are currently available. A list of his written works can be found on page 143.

My thanks to Julia Beard, Geoff Hall and Peter Werbe who read the manuscript and gave me useful comments. My sister, Ruth Nybakken, who, like me, met Fredy in 1957, also read the manuscript. She found a lot to criticize and helped solve numerous problems. I regret that my writing skills do not always satisfy her standards. Ralph Franklin shared his knowledge of the graphic arts and also designed the cover, using a photo furnished by Carl Smith and a woodcut made by John Ricklefs.

I am grateful to Dolores Cherella and William Donovan who gave me loving hospitality and expert advice during many sojourns in the northern suburbs. Marilyn Gilbert and Jeff Gilbert, Fredy's and my close friends since 1970, offered affection and encouragement on Detroit's southwest side. The words and deeds of Mary Jane Shoultz and Federico Arcos brightened my life. My admiration and gratitude go to the dozens of creative individuals in "the Fifth Estate circle" with whom I shared, over the years, contestation and enjoyment in the Motor City. Some of the long-term participants are: Alan Franklin, David Watson, Marilyn Werbe, Marilynn Rashid, Peter Werbe and Ralph Franklin. To these six as well as to all the others, I apologize for the reductive label.

I also want to thank the many unnamed friends residing in Detroit, North America, Europe and Africa who lived part of these years with me and Fredy. He treasured their friendship and acknowledged its decisive impact on his life. I recognize it too and in these pages have tried to honor those who offered it. I should point out, nevertheless, that this is *my* memoir, not theirs.

—*L.P.*

One

The Family

Fredy, the first child of Martha, née Grünberg, and Henry Perlman, was born on August 20, 1934 in Brno, Czechoslovakia. The infant's mother was 24, the father, 29; they had been married the previous October. The Hollywood movie star Fred MacMurray apparently was the source of the name given to the child. But "Fred" must have sounded rather ponderous, even alien, in the newly-established home, and "Fredi" became the accepted version of the infant Perlman's name. (In Bolivia, when he started school, the boy was taught to spell his name "Fredy" and he retained this spelling throughout his life.) On October 30, 1937, in Bratislava, a second son, Peter, was born to Martha and Henry.

Czech was the language spoken in the Perlman home; both parents were equally fluent in German. Martha had attended school when classes were conducted in Czech, while Henry's schooling had been during the final years of the Austro-Hungarian regime when instruction was in German. Henry also spoke Yiddish. In the decades ahead, when they lived in Bolivia and the United States, both Martha and Henry became fluent in Spanish and English. They spoke to each other and the children in the language of the country in which they lived, although Henry frequently employed German or Czech phrases when he had difficulty in expressing himself.

Fredy was his mother's son. Both liked and disliked the same foods; he shared her penchant for silly jokes, had similar ailments. From Martha he learned about her youth, what she studied and the prizes she won in "cooking school" (something like "finishing school"), about her sister and children, Fredy's cousins. He was interested in the family's background; while in grade school, he collected and labeled the photographs his parents had brought from Europe.

Martha no doubt also told Fredy about his paternal ancestors who came from a less affluent milieu, Fredy's paternal grandfather having emigrated to Czechoslovakia from Poland. But Henry was the one who described the poverty of his childhood and his father's lack of economic skills. The oldest of four children, Henry had been obliged to assume the family responsibilities that his father had refused. Henry had a single explanation for his father's shortcomings: Fredy's grand-father had kept his nose in the Talmud and had considered prayers and erudition more important than the family's well-being. (Before Fredy was twenty, both he and his father recognized that Fredy's chosen path was closer to the grandfather's than to the father's.)

As a youth, Henry rejected all religious affiliations and, as far as I know, avoided connections with Jewish institutions throughout his life. Henry became a businessman, initially a representative for a European firm. He traveled a good deal in Central Europe and became familiar with the region. In the 1930s he opened a business of his own. It was a small clothing factory which employed ten or twelve workers. Economic geography was one of the few subjects on which Fredy and his father had non-controversial discussions. Henry could name the capitals of twentieth-century nation-states, knew the history of Europe and was well informed about resources, languages and religions in many parts of the world.

Unlike Martha who had a sentimental, dreamy side to her character and who was a discerning judge of people, Henry rarely deviated from a businessman's interpretation of the world. He judged his profession to be fundamental to social harmony and, if challenged, insisted that he was fulfilling an essential function by transferring goods from producer to consumer. All his energy was directed to his commercial enterprise. His inflexibility was sometimes hard for Martha to take and she resisted by being whimsical, complaining about her health, and objecting to the unvaried routine. She was a meticulous housekeeper who spent part of each day cleaning the house or apart-ment. As the only woman in a household with three males, she sometimes played the role of silly, "ignorant" female. But in fact, she served as an astute business partner to her husband. Although their post-Czechoslovakia enterprises were extremely modest, Martha's judgments were invaluable to their success.

As I observed the domestic dramas which unfolded during our visits with Fredy's parents, my sympathy initially lay with Henry. His opinions seemed sensible and I appreciated his firmness and organized approach (since my family home was always quite anarchic, with all activities and schedules called into question each day). But I came to see that the organization was just rigidity and the reasonable approach was nothing more than following long-established precedents. Once, as we were entering a cafeteria for a meal, Henry warned all of us to beware of choosing something unfamiliar, "You can't be sure what's in some of the things you see here." (Fredy proceeded to choose hominy, okra and a dish with a fluorescent sauce.) Another time in a discussion about socialism, Henry sought to clinch his argument by denouncing Lenin who, when he died, didn't leave his wife so much as a pair of shoes. "Impossible to take seriously the theories of such a man!"

When Fredy came to read Wilhelm Reich's analysis of the individual armored against his own nature, Fredy saw that his father fit Reich's prototype. In many of his own texts Fredy debunked his father's principles, such as: the rule-follower will be rewarded; the non-conformist is a threat to society; all other concerns are secondary to economic security. Rebellion against his father did not preoccupy Fredy or structure his choices, although it was clear to both that the son continued to reject the father's way of life.

It was less clear to Henry whether his second son, Peter, accepted or rejected the precepts offered him. Pete's choices fit into no mold that the father understood: He played baseball, was indifferent to books, had numerous, constantly-changing friends, traveled around the country to attend sports events, ridiculed his parents' grammatical errors and their accent, made jokes about everything. From his youth, Pete was a typical American, a role he took seriously and carried out with gusto and success.

While attending the University of Kentucky, Pete was president of the YMCA and the student governing body. Fredy thought his brother had the personality and the skills to become a professional politician, but Pete did not follow this path. Rather, he concentrated his efforts on becoming a successful and nationally recognized trial lawyer. Martha and Henry were proud of Pete's achievements, appreciated and loved Pete's wife Lana and their three daughters, but were conscious that their "old world" background distanced them from the fashionable, consumer-oriented lifestyle practiced by Pete and his family.

Fredy and Pete remained on friendly terms even though they rarely saw each other and didn't correspond. Fredy was awed by his brother's abilities to please people and did not judge harshly Pete's eagerness to be liked. He observed that Pete, in all social exchanges, used his ability to empathize with and please the person he was talking to; his responses seemed automatic. Fredy wondered if Pete had a coherent perspective of his own. Fredy's views were both fixed and coherent; unlike Pete, he was always eager to propound them.

Neither Fredy nor Pete felt an obligation to make choices their parents would approve of. When he was eighteen, Fredy left his parents' home and supported himself economically. He proudly returned the occasional gifts of money which they offered him.

Two

Reluctant Emigrés

An affection for Czechoslovakia remained a common bond between Fredy and his parents. Sometimes on visits to Cincinnati the four of us would sing Czech songs, among them the national anthem. The songs and words evoked nostalgic memories. Henry often cried. Although he considered himself an American and praised American "know-how," I think he had regrets for the life he might have led in Czechoslovakia, the life of the upstanding Central European citizen, fluent in the region's languages and recognized for his contribution to society.

Martha felt more comfortable in American society than her husband did, but when comparing conventions of everyday life to those in Czechoslovakia, she often judged American ones to be inferior. Martha's appreciation of European comforts and habits was restrained, however. The people who practiced the ways she approved of also permitted the madness that prevailed for a decade. Martha left Czechoslovakia as a young woman of 28, and never again heard from her mother, sister, nephew or niece, victims of the mass murderers who had been nurtured in a society which prided itself on a superior European culture.

It was Henry who chose emigration. In 1939, with their two children, both under five years of age, he and Martha left Czechoslovakia by train. Taking money out of the country was prohibited, but they did it illegally, sewing it in coat linings.

Later that year, with neither a visa nor a specific destination, the Perlman family took a boat from France to Panama. Henry visited embassies there, but none was issuing immigration visas. Finally, an official at the Ecuadorian embassy, acting as representative for another South American republic, offered to sell Henry an immigration visa to Bolivia.

Fredy liked to describe the arrival of his family at the Bolivian border.* The border guards studied the paper Henry handed them. Apparently they couldn't read what was written on it, but they saw an embossed seal and were satisfied that the bearer was worthy of crossing the border. Henry's brother and two sisters, heeding their older brother's advice, emigrated a few weeks later. They and their spouses also made Bolivia their home.

Henry settled his family in the country's second city, Cochabamba, in those days a small town where chickens were kept in courtyards, other animals roamed the streets and the Quechuas came from the highlands to sell produce at the marketplace. Bolivia was not the "America" Henry sought for himself and his family, but since he was unable to get a visa for the United States, he opened a small store in Cochabamba, prepared to wait for the end of the war when he expected his U.S. immigration request to be granted.

Fredy later referred to Spanish as his "first language" but between four and eleven he spoke and understood German and Czech as well. There was a fairly large European community in Cochabamba. It was not exclusively a Jewish group although all shared anti-fascist sentiments. At the frequent picnics and gatherings for festive occasions, people played accordions, sang and danced. Fredy had vivid memories of one such occasion when he was chased by a llama.

In preparation for the hoped-for move to the United States, the parents sent their sons to a school which featured an American teacher. (Fredy remembered the teacher but, except for a few songs, didn't remember learning much English.) The school was private and secular. While a student there, Fredy won a prize for correctly identifying a number of classical musical themes. He also learned the multiplication tables; the Spanish version always seemed more natural to him.

In 1945, the awaited visas were granted and the four Perlmans took a Grace Line freighter to the United States. They were obliged

---

*He claimed to have remembered it himself, but even if he did, the interpretation seems to be Henry's.

to disembark at the first U.S. port—an inauspicious one, Mobile, Alabama. The Bolivian peso had been repeatedly devalued, so by 1945 the dollar sum Henry got when he sold his Cochabamba store was a pittance. Henry had begun studying English before their arrival, but discovered with dismay that he could understand nothing of the language spoken around him. He succeeded in finding work in Mobile but, whether by a local resident's ignorance or perverse sense of humor, he was hired as a salesman in a downtown department store. When customers approached him to ask where certain items were located, Henry was humiliated to have to admit that he couldn't even understand the questions. Decades later he could treat the experience with some detachment: "I didn't know if they were asking for toilet paper or sandpaper."

Discouraged about career prospects in Mobile, Henry took his family to New York City. Here, especially on the lower east side of Manhattan, he found people with whom he could converse and who willingly helped him get established in American commercial life. His first endeavor was exceedingly modest—a "candy store" in Brooklyn. He and Martha sold comic books, ice cream, soda pop and candy to the neighborhood residents, mostly the youth. Henry called the adolescents "hoodlums" because they teased him, called him familiarly by his first name and laughed at his difficulties with English. Martha was extremely unhappy here, regretting the comforts and more civilized clientele they had known in Europe and Bolivia.

In less than two years, Henry sold the candy store, the family moved to a home in Queens and the parents operated a variety store in the fast-growing suburb of Hollis, Long Island.

Fredy's companion and closest friend in Queens was a boy Fredy's parents disapproved of. The principal activity the two youths shared was bicycling down the newly-laid runways of Idlewild—later Kennedy—airport, but Sonny was frequently "in trouble." There were accusations that he stole bikes from the school parking lot. Many of Sonny's confidences and escapades found their way into *Letters of Insurgents* in the character of Ron. Already in the 1940s, Fredy told Sonny he would write a book about him.

Fredy attended public schools in New York City. In the fall of 1948 he became a ninth grade student at Brooklyn Technical High School. To get to and from school, he had to spend two hours a day on the subway and bus.

When Fredy was fifteen, he and his family moved to Lakeside Park, Kentucky, a suburb of Cincinnati, Ohio. Martha and Henry bought a large variety store which they operated from 1949 to 1966. In those years, the high school Fredy attended was a melting pot for students coming from a Baptist/Christian, essentially rural, background and students from a more urban milieu. The new environment was quite different from metropolitan New York, but Fredy made efforts and was successful at integrating himself. He worked on the school newspaper, played cymbals in the band and won a television set as a prize in a state essay contest ("I speak for democracy") writing as a refugee from Europe's racism. Coming from an upper-track NYC high school, he was scornful of Lakeside Park's teaching staff. He obviously spoke Spanish better than the Spanish teacher and Fredy claimed that the math teacher (whose more important position was Coach) couldn't even copy the problems correctly from the book.

Viewed from the 1980s, high school social life in the 1950s was quite innocent. There was almost no alcohol consumption and certainly no drugs. But it was still a time of personal tragedies. One of Fredy's fellow students committed suicide because his love for a beautiful girl in their class was rejected.

In the Kentucky setting where urban and rural outlooks came together, religious affiliation was a central part of one's identity. For part of a year Fredy attended meetings of a youth group at a Cincinnati temple. He was the only member of his family to associate with a Jewish organization. In later years he justified his brief affiliation by explaining that the rabbi, leader of the group, was a peace and civil rights activist.

When he was sixteen, Fredy got a car. (Not until several years later did either of his parents learn to drive.) He was part of a circle of friends who drove around in cars and visited each other's homes where they listened to records; Stan Kenton and Bartok recordings were ones Fredy mentioned as favorites.

Fredy used his car to get to Cincinnati where he worked part-time as stock boy for a wholesale merchant. It was here that Fredy learned the "professional" packing skills that he continued to apply in the Detroit print shop and in sending out Black & Red publications. In this and subsequent jobs, Fredy was a conscientious employee rather than the inherently rebellious worker he admired among his associates and depicted approvingly in his writing. He did not take advantage of opportunities to cheat his employer of time or goods.

Except for the academic job which he held a decade later, Fredy accepted the structure and the rules of the workplace. In fact, he often used techniques learned on the job in his own activities as when, for example, he packed books, washed dishes or organized a routine at a printing press. Fredy nevertheless was no "ideal worker." He scorned the person whose identity was defined by and limited to his or her work function. Fredy never subordinated his needs to the "needs" of the employer and he refused to tolerate any superior who practiced arbitrary authority. A significant number of Fredy's jobs ended with abrupt resignations.

Three

Fredy Leaves Home

In 1951, against his parents' wishes, Fredy went to New York to spend the summer in Queens with Sonny, his "hoodlum" buddy. He worked in a fiberglass factory and discovered the hazards associated with industrial production as well as workers' acquiescence to their situation.

In the fall he returned to Kentucky and graduated from high school the following spring. His first year in college was at a state school in Morehead, Kentucky. He had a tuition scholarship from the college; to pay living expenses he took part-time jobs as a janitor and as an assistant in the school's public relations office. Morehead was in backwoods Kentucky and Fredy humorously described his initial difficulties in communicating with some of the local inhabitants.

The professors who influenced him most were Europeans: a dynamic Italian woman who taught French and a German professor of history; the latter provided Fredy with a model of a multi-faceted intellectual. This man invited students to his home; in addition to listening to the professor's complaints about provincial Morehead, the student guests listened to classical music. Both European teachers found the small-town environment restrictive and Fredy came to share their view. In the summer of 1953 he headed for Los Angeles by car.

Fredy enjoyed telling about his arriving broke in Los Angeles and going to sleep on the beach after spending his last 25 cents on coffee and cigarettes. After finding a gardening job which furnished room and board, he went to the school newspaper office at the University of California at Los Angeles (UCLA). His arrival caused a stir among some of the worldly-wise staff members. They were impressed by the courage and audacity of a naive youth from Kentucky who just showed up in the *Daily Bruin* office.

Fredy's two years in Los Angeles had an enormous influence on his future outlook; this dramatic period continued to serve as a point of reference. Within days of his arrival he became a UCLA student and joined the staff of the *Daily Bruin.* He took courses given by prestigious professors, but whatever he learned in classes was filtered through his experiences on the newspaper.

Los Angeles, and particularly UCLA, was one of the theaters for the McCarthy witch-hunts of the 1950s. The repression threatened the very circles Fredy found stimulating. During the term when Fredy was copy editor, editorials in the *Daily Bruin* ridiculed the patriots' paranoia and defended constitutionally guaranteed civil liberties. Interviews with professors under attack by the witch-hunters gave the accused a chance to defend their views. Anti-communist faculty members were also interviewed; one of them attributed all the country's and the university's problems to "Baltic Jews." In the smear campaign mounted by the Los Angeles newspapers, the *Daily Bruin* was frequently cited as proof that UCLA had become "the little red schoolhouse." In December 1954 the university regents imposed new regulations on the newspaper; the staff members who refused to accept the directive were fired. All five editors as well as the majority of their co-workers denounced the restrictions and left the paper.

In fact, none of the five *Bruin* editors were spokesmen for a radical party or ideology. They disagreed on many issues, but they all had a libertarian perspective and were not easily intimidated. They scrupulously adhered to the principles of responsible journalism while finding it natural to use their wit to debunk the growing anti-communist fervor and their writing skills to warn of its implications. When the directive was imposed, these articulate and intelligent students sought an appropriate response. One response was to organize a large funeral cortege mourning the death of the *Daily Bruin,* an act which anticipated some of the creative demonstrations of a decade later. Another response was to publish an alternative newspaper which conformed to their principles. This activity created even stronger bonds between the dozen or so individuals who had previously published the *Daily Bruin.* The months of intense activity in early 1955 remained a decisive juncture for most of the participants in the *Observer* project. In *Letters*

of Insurgents, written twenty years later, Fredy tried to recreate the
anxiety and concerns of this period.

These experiences gave him insights about the gulf that separated
him and his comrades from the fraternity and sorority milieu (these
students refused to accept the free *Observer* handed out on street
corners facing the campus entrance) and about the potency of established institutions. The formerly respected journalists, providers of
information to the student body, abruptly found themselves to be outsiders, criminals to a few, cranks to many. As proud as they were
of themselves for being true to their principles, the ousted staff realized
that the *Observer* could not compete with the *Daily Bruin.* Besides
losing their salaries as staff members, they had to subsidize the
Observer's publication and do without the university's equipment and
resources. None of the participants regretted their defiance of the
university's directives but they may not all have drawn the same conclusion as Fredy who thereafter consciously shunned institutional
roles—suspicious of those who wielded institutional authority and
hostile to those who respected it.

Looking back, Fredy had a few regrets about the *Observer*
experiences. There were five editors—all of them men. The hierarchy of a conventional newspaper staff was never questioned. The
women participants may have worked just as hard, but they received
less recognition. One of the tasks delegated to non-editors was the
distribution of the paper, a task which may not always have been
pleasant. The typing of the paper, however, was done by one of the
editors—Fredy.

While in Los Angeles, Fredy learned to play the guitar; he was
motivated by the folk singing and folk dancing sessions he attended.
In his circle of friends there were a number of Communist Party
members. The erudition of some of them and the coherence of their
arguments impressed him. But he scorned their adherence to a party.

For a time, Fredy shared an apartment with the son of CP
members. His roommate's parents with whom he became well
acquainted were quite unlike his own; he was enchanted by their enthusiasm and joyfulness. After associating with them, he considered it
essential that a political commitment be combined with enjoyment
of life.

To pay the expenses of an apartment and maintain his car, Fredy
worked part time as a dishwasher in a Mexican restaurant. He learned
to prepare Mexican dishes from the chefs at this restaurant; in future
years his cheese enchiladas would be acclaimed by many guests.

During his last year at UCLA Fredy lived in a campus co-op. As editor of the co-op's mimeographed newspaper, he often vociferously opposed the regulations that the university tried to impose on the autonomous student organization. The majority of the students who shared the facilities worried that their careers could be jeopardized if the group resisted university guidelines, and Fredy's call to defiance was usually rejected. The compromises and toadyism of some of his fellow co-opers disappointed and distressed him. He already considered himself a "radical," and his associates did not disagree.

Fredy's first serious love was a young woman who worked on the *Bruin* and the *Observer*. But she never committed herself and Fredy always had rivals. This experience could be the source for the poignant accounts of thwarted love in his stories (*Letters of Insurgents, The Strait*). Years later, in the 1970s, Fredy's mother had a photo from Fredy's UCLA days propped up in her bedroom—a photo she thought was of me and Fredy. I was shocked to note my resemblance to Jean Fox.

Unrequited love may have been partially responsible for Fredy's departure for Mexico City in 1955. Disappointment with the *Observer* was certainly a factor. He went alone by car and sought new friends. In Mexico City he lived in a *pensión* and associated principally with South American students. Not having a B.A. degree, he could not enroll at the University of Mexico City. During his months in Mexico, he read Latin American history and fiction, he regained facility in speaking Spanish and got acquainted with Mexico City. Having a car, he had a few contacts with people in villages too.

In December 1955, Fredy returned to the United States and enrolled at the University of Kentucky in Lexington. In one semester and a summer term he completed requirements for a B.A. degree. He had to be a conscientious student since one of the Dean's conditions for graduating in 1956 was that Fredy get A's in all his courses. He succeeded.

In the fall of 1956 Fredy went to New York City where he enrolled as a graduate student in English at Columbia University. He had decided to suspend political commitments for a certain time while he explored the offerings of a major university. With his characteristic intensity, Fredy immersed himself in classes and books; when I met him in January 1957 he had no friends in New York.

The ivory tower perspective of the literature professors antagonized him immediately. He had no means of attacking it and his isolation meant that he wasn't even able to communicate his criticisms to others. William York Tindal, a T.S. Eliot scholar, particularly angered him; Fredy accused him of looking only at the form and not at the content of the poet's work.

After a few weeks at Columbia, Fredy realized that the literature professors were not providing him with what he was seeking from the ivy-covered walls and he started attending lectures in many other fields. Courses in philosophy and political science were the ones that particularly stimulated him. This was the material he was hoping to find and he expressed a Faustian urge to familiarize himself with the entire corpus of Western thought.

At 23, Fredy knew he had already chosen an unconventional path. His judgment of the "mediocrity" of UCLA comrades in a letter to Marty McReynolds, a close friend from the *Bruin* and *Observer* projects, elicited a lengthy response. Excerpts from Marty's self-analytic letter follow.

> Dear Fredy,
> . . .
> . . .[I]t disgusts you to hear about the mediocritization of our old friends, but it only makes me a little sad. And partly because I have not yet qualified for their mediocrity and I envy them. . .I always have been pretty middle-class and provincial in my outlook and it wouldn't be surprising if I end up more mediocre and middle-class than anybody, if I can make the grade. But right now I am identity-less. . .I'm not a Fredy with a task before him. And I'm not a mediocrity with his decisions behind him. I'm an indecision hovering between mediocrity and bum. It wouldn't take too much for my natural lethargy to lead me into a sloth-like existence as some kind of bum, but my middle-class conscience would never let me enjoy myself that way.
> . . .
> Remember the last Observer eddy board meeting? You said we had done what we could, and now it was up to someone else to do something. And I didn't like your sad, resigned tone of voice which reminded me of the resignation-to-life which I sensed in the future for myself at least. I said even if we were going to be conformists the rest of our lives, we had stood up once and punched authority in the nose. I seem to see that talk more clearly now. You spoke for yourself, as events have turned out. You left that task to others and went on to something else. I spoke for myself and some of the others, as it now seems. People who spend their lives working to feed and clothe

themselves and their hi-fis, but who once at least stood up and did something not in their own self-interest.

But just because some people once thought and acted, I don't think it's necessarily justifiable to be disgusted when those people seem to "adjust," "grow up" and knuckle down to conformity. What would you have them do? We are all animals, biological beings, and we respond to stimuli on the basis of what is inside of us. You have responded one way—for which you deserve no credit—and others have responded another way—for which they deserve no censure...Anyway, dammit, I wonder if all the mediocrities don't represent a challenge to you and your course of action. You are pretty much incapable of being one of them, which is probably good, but it makes your position different from that of a person who could have happy conformity but chooses something else. I speculate that you would be miserable as a conformist, so you have made no choice, you have done only what you had to do. Others find that they would be miserable if they didn't conform. Each of your positions challenges the other, and maybe that is why you talk about mediocrity in such fierce terms. I know damn well your position challenges mine. And however much I wish you success I will always feel twinges of displeasure as you achieve meaningful goals, even if I am pleased at the same time...

"Mediocrity is not something given to us at birth...we choose it because we couldn't or wouldn't face the fact that we are not what we could be." This hits me squarely. I am not what I could be. But, you know, that really means I am not what I could be IF I had drive, or IF I had direction or some other damn thing...If I turn out to be a typical mediocrity (distinguished only by an eccentric interest in Mexicana which is after all not unusual these days anyway), I may be disgusted with myself. But if I turn out to be satisfied that way, maybe I will stop writing to you and talking to people who remind me there is something else in life besides conformity...

. . .

Look, I'm proud of you. I'm glad of you...Maybe in six months I will forget what I said and rationalize in an entirely different way, well, keep writing and find out.

Marty

During his three years at Columbia, Fredy did not seek any political activists—on the campus or off. Nor did he reevaluate his political outlook which had evolved at UCLA. It lay dormant. Fredy expected to return to earlier, social, concerns but he found this sojourn among the intellectuals to be challenging and engrossing. He admired the philosophers and social analysts whose works he was reading; his appreciation was not uncritical, however, and he constantly tried to pinpoint what in these theories was inadequate for a meaningful interpretation of the contemporary world.

Fredy and I met at the Columbia University Admissions Office in January 1957 where we both had part-time jobs. In February he was obliged to report to the military authorities to have an army physical examination. (In those years, all healthy males were required to serve for two years in the army.) Since his heart had been damaged by rheumatic fever when he was ten years old, Fredy was quite sure he would not pass the physical exam, but in case he should be accepted, he prepared himself to denounce the army and to refuse to sign the loyalty oath required of all recruits. There was no opportunity for the dramatic refusal. The army doctors noted Fredy's heart condition after just a few minutes and sent him away.

Fredy returned to his job operating the Admission Office's automatic typewriters. The conversations he and I began at work soon continued after hours. We did not actually share living quarters until January 1958, but nearly every evening and weekend we were together. We prepared and ate our meals at the Yorkshire rooming house on 113th Street where I lived. Later we both lived there. One morning, before going to our afternoon jobs at the Admissions Office, we went to the Manhattan City Hall and were legally married. This did not coincide with our move to live together. We both had misgivings about linking our lives in a conventional way; one of the main factors in our decision was a desire to be accepted by our parents. In any case, this change in our legal status was not known to anyone else and it was only after we went to Europe in 1963 that I started using Fredy's last name.

We had only a handful of friends in the years at Columbia University. One was a musician friend of mine from high school and college days, an artistic and mystical violinist. Another friend was Zigrida Arbatsky who also worked at the Admissions Office. She and her Russian husband were both emigrés. Yury was a brilliant and outrageous man—a composer, religious philosopher, intellectual—who remained a misfit in the American environment. He may not have been unique, but when I read Vladimir Nabokov's *Pnin*, I was certain the author had Yury Arbatsky in mind.

During three years of intensive study at Columbia University Fredy concentrated on the works of Western philosophers. He was particularly impressed by the political philosophers – Plato, Augustine, Aquinas, Hegel, Locke. He also attended courses in Russian intellectual history and Russian literature. A course on the sociology of literature given by Leo Lowenthal was esteemed by Fredy. Outside of classes he read many of the classics of European literature. Influential authors were Thomas Mann, Goethe, Ibsen, Strindberg, Sartre. Sometimes, especially on summer outings to the beach, we read plays aloud; and we went to performances of European plays. The sociology courses given by C.W. Mills were for undergraduate males but Fredy attentively audited them. He was impressed by Mills's harangues at the students as well as by the material covered. Mills was an *enragé,* searching for an outlet to his anger. In those quiescent days, Mills was remarkable for personally building his own home and for coming to class on a motorcycle. Mills clearly was trying to apply holistic principles to his daily life. Bringing his anger and quest to the "lectures" made them remarkable for Fredy, if not for the undergraduates (who didn't know what to expect on the exams). At the end of the term Fredy approached Mills for advice on meaningful activity in this society. It now seems clear that Mills himself was searching for an answer to that question. The answer Fredy received – contact the American Friends' Service Committee – was disappointing.

Fredy's identification with the Faustian protagonist of so much literature led him to read many versions of the Faust story. He took a course in modern music and listened to classical music – recorded and live – whenever possible. His musical tastes were colored to some extent by his political views. For example, he disliked Charles Ives's compositions, not because of the dissonance or avant-garde techniques (he generally accepted both with an open mind), but because Ives had been a successful businessman. Fredy disapproved of the composer's acceptance of capitalist society's priorities and felt that by suspending creative activity while assuring economic security, Ives had put money before art.

He read and admired the novels and plays of Sartre and Camus and took a course in Existentialism given by R.D. Cumming, one of the professors whose course in political philosophy he had found valuable. Czeslaw Milosz's *The Captive Mind* and Arthur Koestler's *Darkness at Noon* had a sobering impact on any enthusiasm he may have had for a benign regime headed by either a philosopher-king or an omniscient party.

Fredy included science in his Faustian endeavor to acquaint himself with Western thought. During the months when Sputnik was in the headlines, we were both enrolled in courses in physics and calculus at the City College of New York.

One day Fredy abruptly quit his job at the Admissions Office. The Director, demanding certain tasks of Fredy, had made it clear that as operator of the typing machines, Fredy was no more than an extension of the office equipment. Fredy soon found another job as switchboard operator in a resident hotel. He worked the night shift, three times a week. The job had definite shortcomings, but provided several uninterrupted hours for reading. At his job during these months Fredy read Arnold Toynbee's *A Study of History,* a work he valued highly. Fredy often referred to the various non-Western civilizations he had learned about from Toynbee, even though he disagreed with the historian's Christian interpretation.

Four

The Unattached Intellectual in New York

In the summer of 1959 Fredy felt it was time to leave the university. On a motorscooter we set out on what became a three and a half month trip from New York City to the West Coast and back. We carried tent, sleeping bag, cooking utensils and clothes on the back of our Lambretta 125. Our maximum traveling speed (downhill) was 35 miles per hour. In 1959 the network of freeways had not yet been built but we would have avoided them even if they had been available.

In order to cross the continent twice we obviously had to spend several hours a day on the scooter. On this trip we saw the country, not cities or people; we usually chose secondary roads. Almost every night we slept in the tent and cooked supper over a wood fire at a campground or park. The weather was naturally important to us, and Fredy, the urban intellectual, learned to predict which clouds threatened to dump their contents on us.

Rain slowed us down, but didn't deter us. In fact, we saw a good part of the Columbia River Valley through the rain. We were practically the only tourists in Yellowstone Park (where we rented a cabin due to the cold temperatures); other travelers avoided it because of an earthquake a week earlier. In two California parks — Yosemite and Sequoia — bears roamed the campgrounds at night. In the latter park, noises outside the tent woke us one October night when we were alone in a campground. It was a bear taking our clothing bag (which, through an oversight, contained an apple) from under a picnic table to the edge of the surrounding woods where he/she neatly cut the bag along the zipper, took possession of the apple and disappeared.

Heading east out of the Grand Canyon, we drove into a blizzard and were rescued from highway hazards and the cold by a sympathetic man who was traveling to the eastern border of Arizona. He carried us in the cab of his pickup truck and the scooter in the back. In Texas we did not always find campgrounds. One night we stayed in a barn. The caretaker of this isolated ranch readily gave us permission to sleep there and in the morning prepared a generous breakfast for us. To eat it, Fredy and I shared the man's single fork. Our host was more interested in talking than in eating and didn't need silverware to drink his beer.

On Thanksgiving Day we arrived at my parents' home in Iowa City with only pennies left. On a subsequent scooter trip we traveled through Wisconsin, Michigan's upper peninsula, central Ontario, a corner of Quebec, Maine and rural New England. We retained from these travels an appreciation of the vastness and natural wonders of the continent.

Returning to New York in December 1959, Fredy felt he was ready to synthesize what he had learned from books, travel and experiences. We took an apartment on Henry Street on the lower east side of Manhattan. Residents of New York feel that their city is the center of the world. Fredy felt vital and ready to challenge the American Way of Life from the belly of the monster's most important city.

Fredy hoped that his analysis of the ideological trappings and inequitable social relations would lead to the downfall of the profit-oriented, racist, militaristic rulers of the country. His project was to transmit a human-centered vision. In these days he counted heavily on the rationality of the individual who, when informed, would choose socially responsible alternatives rather than the selfish, nationalistic ones proposed and imposed by manipulative leaders. Arguments acquired from Erich Fromm and Lewis Mumford, as well as Mary and Charles Beard's historical analysis of the United States, were incorporated in his critique of post-war American society. *I.F. Stone's Weekly* kept him informed about the machinations of contemporary politicians. Fredy may already have read Marx's *Capital* but I think any Marxist analysis he had in the years on Henry Street was limited to what came from his reading and assimilating *The Communist Manifesto* as well as from *Monthly Review* authors. Fredy had great respect for the books and articles of Paul Baran and Paul Sweezy.

He read and saved all the *New York Times*. Looking back, this astonishes me since after 1963, I think he read no more than one newspaper per year. He listened to most of the United Nations debates. This was the period following the Cuban Revolution and the CIA-instigated coup in the Congo carried out after the radical African nationalist Patrice Lumumba was assassinated. Fredy accepted the U.N. speakers as legitimate spokesmen of their countries' national interest and considered their debates to have an influence on international politics.

Fredy abandoned the study of science. Other concerns were more pressing. He thought that if the political forms could be changed, the aims of science would be directed away from military ends and its integrity restored. He was appalled by the noxious achievements of science: nuclear weaponry and the outrages against natural processes documented in Robert Jungk's *Tomorrow is Already Here.* Scientists' subservience to military authority permitted the increasingly efficacious violence to be wielded more impersonally. Fredy read the *Bulletin of Atomic Scientists* (a journal which first appeared in the early 1960s), hoping that scientists who contributed articles might provide a way to counter the baffling renunciation of responsibility. Fredy wanted scientists to retain control over uses to which their research was put. He believed these men and women would use it for less harmful ends.

In the three years we lived on the lower east side of Manhattan Fredy earned a subsistence income doing free-lance mimeographing and typing.* This was before the proliferation of quick-copy stores, and Fredy found customers among the academic, religious and commercial residents in the area. Throughout most of the year he was able to deliver the copies by motorscooter.

We followed cultural events and went to museums, plays, concerts and films. Our modest income made restaurant meals the exception rather than commonplace. Both Fredy and I were content with our material situation, considering it appropriate that artistic and political bohemians live on the fringes.

The biggest change in our lives was that the isolation of the Columbia years ended. We had a growing circle of friends. They were concerned, vigorous individuals; many had creative interests.

---

*After an initial attempt (which lasted four months) to establish an enterprise in a storefront on Sixth Street, the work was done in our fifth floor walk-up apartment.

Besides his interest in printing and literature, Fredy grew to appreciate the efforts of musicians, painters and sculptors as well as practitioners of the theatrical arts.

Our neighbors on Henry Street were a young Swiss couple who had recently arrived in New York. Daily life in lower Manhattan did not conform to the glittering image of America projected abroad, and they had no trouble pointing to ways in which, compared to Europeans, Americans were impoverished. They were surprised that New Yorkers were so tolerant of the poor quality of food, the noise and dirt in the subway and the dismal urban landscapes. But the widespread fear of ideological deviation shocked them more than anything else. Claire worked in an office at the United Nations among people with somewhat cosmopolitan attitudes. But Jean-Jacques's fellow workers, house painters earning the minimum wage, were afraid that Jean-Jacques, the newcomer who spoke with an accent unlike theirs, might not originate from the "free world." They were relieved to learn that Switzerland belonged to "our" side.

Jean-Jacques earned money painting walls of apartments. As an artist, he assembled articles he found in trash heaps, juxtaposing inharmonious pieces in "objects" which he hoped would communicate his observations about the society in which they originated. Neither Jean-Jacques nor Claire was "political" when they came to the U.S. in 1961. Their interests were in film, art and literature. After living in New York for five years, their distaste for American society had grown enormously. The "political" statement with which they responded to their almost complete alienation was to emigrate to Cuba.

A friend from UCLA spent a lot of time with us in our first year on Henry Street. He had been a member of the Communist Party's youth group, but after Khrushchev's revelations in 1956, Gene had rejected communism and all political activity. This young man of 25 felt he had sacrificed career possibilities to militant activity during his student years, and he harbored deep resentment toward those who had "misled" him. In 1960 he turned from the attempt to overthrow bourgeois society to the study of Eastern religion, and his readings furnished him with arguments to justify his efforts to avoid worldly activities. Thanks to a sympathetic friend, he was eventually able to live as caretaker on a formerly elegant estate in upstate New York. Fredy's depiction of this dropout-victim in *Letters of Insurgents* is perhaps unkind, but hardly exaggerated.

For an intense period lasting several weeks, Fredy and two friends, Saul Gottlieb and Frances Witlin, worked together formulating

principles for a new political party. In their discussions, which often
lasted through the night, they tried to resolve many of the dilemmas
which arise when the choices of individuals conflict with an enlightened representative's understanding of what is best for the society.
They also discussed economic questions; their attempt to formulate
a coherent program at least partially motivated Fredy's later study
of world resources. As far as I know, no outline or written conclusions remain from this collective undertaking.

Protest actions organized by people around the Living Theatre
broadened the circle of friends and provided a sense of community.
From 1947 until 1965 when they moved to Europe, the Living Theatre
presented the most stimulating and relevant dramatic productions in
New York (probably in the U.S.) and introduced works by B. Brecht,
J. Gelber and W.C. Williams to a wide audience. The founders of
the Living Theatre, Judith Malina and Julian Beck, were militant
pacifists and spoke of themselves as anarchists. They were as profi-
cient at civil disobedience actions as they were in theatrical endeavors.
In 1955 they had been arrested for refusing to take shelter during
an air raid drill. In 1962 the IRS closed their theater because they
had withheld federal taxes.

Public demonstrations in the early 1960s focused on the frequent
testing of nuclear weapons and the government's continuing militaristic
build-up. Quakers held vigils and called for the public to disavow
U.S. policies. The Fair Play for Cuba Committee organized demonstrations; these were usually held at the U.N. and called for American
and other national rulers to accept the Cuban leaders as their peers.

The most lively protests were those organized by the Living
Theatre group. They raised broader social issues and civil disobedience was often part of the confrontation. Fredy joined Judith, Julian
and others in a number of attempts to disrupt bourgeois society's daily
routine at the N.Y. Stock Exchange and in Times Square. Though
small in numbers they felt they were communicating their views.

At one Times Square demonstration Fredy and dozens of others
were arrested when they sat down in the street and disrupted traffic.
After a grim night in jail, they were released on bond. Their trial
was postponed a number of times and Fredy resented the time spent
worrying about the outcome as well as the time spent in the
courtroom—another form of legal harassment, he called it. One result
of the delays was that Fredy became well acquainted with the three
other defendants who appeared on the same docket. Months after
the Times Square demonstration, they were given suspended
sentences.

Many of the individuals attracted to Living Theatre activities—the transition generation between the Beats and the hippies—had rejected society's norms to a much greater extent than Fredy had. Although he liked the people he met at these gatherings, he was not tempted to take them as models. Fredy thought a systematic analysis of the social and economic system was a prerequisite for fundamental change; the apolitical interests of many of these friends caused him to keep his distance.

His critique of the Quaker wing of the anti-war movement was more severe. These middle-class and often affluent professionals demonstrated against U.S. militarism but often defended institutions that Fredy considered repressive. At times they had a condescending attitude toward demonstrators like us who came from outside the Quaker tradition, as if to imply that our anti-military fervor was less genuine than theirs.

It was in Quaker circles that Fredy met John Ricklefs, a man of his age but with an entirely different background and history. From 1960 to 1962 John and Fredy collaborated on projects in New York, and they continued one of them in Belgrade. John and Fredy quickly became close friends and spent many hours together every day. They had long, discursive, eclectic discussions about appropriate means of communication and about economic geography, music, food and architecture. When they undertook a study of world resources, their discussions became more focused, but they tried to make the scope of their research all-inclusive.

John had grown up in Kansas. On graduation from the university as an architect, he became an ROTC officer in the air force and was assigned to the Security Air Command base in northern New York state. While there, he became disaffected with the military and realized that he would be unable to carry out his duties in an "emergency." Communicating his disaffection to his superiors, an early discharge was negotiated.

John and his literary wife Margery, both vegetarians, came to Manhattan in 1960 where they transformed a loft on 24th Street into elegant living quarters. As a job, John prepared landscaping plans for an architect who designed parking lots and freeways. John was an artist too: he painted abstract expressionist canvases and made expressive wood sculptures, often depicting hands.

John and Fredy met at an opportune time for both. John was questioning many of the tenets which underlay his view of the world. Fredy's articulate formulation of ideas, his knowledge of political philosophy and his intense desire to understand and change society made John want to emulate him. Fredy welcomed John's insights about creativity and social planning, and he immediately incorporated John's experiences into his analyses. Both John and Fredy had read and appreciated the books of Lewis Mumford when they met in 1960.

Fredy was a demanding friend, especially in those years. He did not want a disciple, but required consensus on many issues before work on a common project could proceed. He had inexhaustible energy when defending his views. In discussions he could always find apt analogies and cite historical precedents. He rarely used ridicule to argue against someone's objections, but depended on his conviction that the force of his logic would prevail. Generally it did. Nevertheless, Fredy's exceptional endurance rarely hindered his cause.

Fredy's historical essay, *The New Freedom: Corporate Capitalism,* preceded the study undertaken with John. In it Fredy analyzes contemporary U.S. society and traces inequities back to explicit intentions of the founding fathers. The essay uses Charles and Mary Beard's economic history to emphasize the fact that the United States has been a class society from its origins. Fredy denounces Alexander Hamilton and his colleagues for cheating the yeomen and artisans of their share of social wealth. He points out that government and business have always worked together to further the interests of the rich and wellborn who, in the twentieth century, have become increasingly anonymous—their administrative functions now being carried out by corporations. In *The New Freedom,* Fredy suggests that one remedy for the inequities, waste and militarism would be for the underclass (workers) to rise and assert their rights to manage the productive facilities and legislative institutions. The Cuban Revolution is offered as a reasonable response to an oppressive government.

John was an enthusiastic collaborator on *The New Freedom,* furnishing five large woodcuts in two or three colors, as well as dozens of smaller, one-color woodcuts. Once Fredy had mimeographed the 91 copies of the text (201 single-spaced typed pages), he and John imprinted the woodcuts by hand in John's loft; they hung the pages on clotheslines to dry. Binding the book was another labor-intensive process. First the five sections were stapled, then taped together, and the large woodprints attached at the juncture of the sections. Finally the cover and spine (with title) were glued. Binding a single book took a lot of time. My sister, Ruth Nybakken, often came to help us. As we worked, we listened to programs on WBAI, the newly-established non-commercial radio station.

In publishing his first book himself, Fredy intentionally avoided commercial media. He conceived of this work as a gift, not a commodity. In its opening pages, John and Fredy challenge the reader to widen the network of non-business communication. Fredy never revised these principles on transmitting written words; over the years he made the challenge in many forms—but usually less judgementally and with less urgency than in *The New Freedom*. Before the title page, one finds this note:

Reader,

At the hazard of being dismissed by you we imprudently ask you to undertake certain obligations on receiving this book. Prudence, we feel, is not the proper response to impending catastrophe which, if it is to be averted, had better be met with acute foresight, with critical appraisal, with courageous action.

The book is addressed to what the author considers the critical problems of all Humanity in our time. The problems are the current misery of mankind, and the threat of a genocidal war. The misery cannot be alleviated, nor the destruction averted, by men who are not conscious of the threat or of its causes.

The purpose of this book is to communicate the author's understanding of these problems to readers. We feel convinced that such communication cannot be accomplished by a publishing network whose primary purpose is not communication but profit.

In view of these considerations, we turn to you, reader, and ask you to make yourself responsible for the life or the death, the enjoyment or the misery, of all humanity. We ask this by placing a small task before you, a task which is not intended to be the end of your endeavors, but merely the cue which we hope will inspire you to devise far greater projects of your own.

We do not ask you to agree with the analysis contained in this book, in whole or in part; but we do ask you to read the book, and to share at least our concern.

We further ask you to share our concern over the lack of unfettered media of communication in a land where the press is a business. You and I are, we feel, responsible to devise ways of circumventing this lack. We want you to join us in a search for a free press and a free literature whose sole aim is communication.

If you share our concern, if not our interpretation, we ask you either to see to it that this book is reproduced again, and yet again, and distributed without charge, or that your own interpretation of the problem is reproduced and distributed free of charge. If you do this, reader, the business press will have been circumvented.

If you feel yourself better suited to different forms of communication, allow us to suggest free plays, free novels, posters, pamphlets; allow us to suggest that you organize your community for lectures, forums, pickets, strikes. . .

If you do none of these things, and if you do not engage yourself in any of the infinite number of projects which have not occurred to us, then know, reader, that in our eyes you will have abdicated your responsibility to all living humanity, and to all the dead who have made you what you are, given you what you have, and taught you what you know.

Fredy Perlman
John E. Ricklefs

Fredy wrote the play *Plunder* in 1962. At the time, he was participating in many Living Theatre activities and probably hoped the theater collective would perform it. The work provides an overview of corporate evil in action outside the U.S.: wars, economic distress, racism. An American businessman-imperialist with nineteenth-century attitudes and his four more modern sons are the principal characters. Three of the sons carry on their father's project in southern Africa and Asia: One is a Marine who turns to war when the populace rejects his authority; another is an economic "developer" who ruins the local artisans; the third is a modern bureaucrat whose administrative decrees destroy the very fabric of traditional society. The drama is furnished by the progressive unmasking of the good intentions of these sons of imperialism. The play is "staged" by a fourth son who repudiates any solidarity with his family of devastators. (This son's name is Bruno, chosen to link Fredy's fervent denouncer with the sixteenth-century martyr-enlightener.)

In the 1970s when printing facilities were readily accessible, Fredy reprinted *Plunder*, but he never reprinted *The New Freedom*. By then he had changed many opinions expressed in these two works. I think he valued *Plunder* as a work which transcends a flat denunciation of imperialism and he still considered Bruno's eloquent wrath to be an appropriate response to human-induced injustice.

Five

A 'Definitive' Departure from the U.S.

In October 1962, nationalism and war hysteria gripped the United States when it was learned that Soviet missiles had been installed in Cuba. Most Americans regarded the installation as an act of war. Newspapers depicted Fidel Castro, Cuba's prime minister, as an arrogant, vengeful monster, and the Soviet rulers as scheming devils keen to have weapons within ninety miles of the "free world's" heartland. President Kennedy's threat to bomb Cuba was greeted with warm approval in the media and by most New Yorkers.

Fredy and I took part in some of the demonstrations which were organized to protest against U.S. intervention in Cuba, but they had little effect on either the government or public opinion. Patriotic citizens were all too willing to prove their loyalty by beating up the protestors (largely pacifists) but the police took care to keep the two groups separated. Most passers-by considered us Communist dupes and hurled invective.

The hate-filled atmosphere and the feeling that we were unable to change anything made escape seem an appealing alternative. Comments by subway riders who proposed that "We bomb Cuba off the face of the earth" made Fredy feel he could not continue to live in the belly of the beast, and we made plans to go to Europe.

Although we got our passports right away, almost three months passed before we actually left. Since we thought we were leaving the U.S. for good, we disposed of all our possessions except for those that fit in a large foot locker. For several weeks we both worked full-time jobs; Fredy was employed as a printer; he operated a multilith press in a midtown Manhattan print shop.

John Ricklefs, too, decided to leave the country. The recent break-up of his marriage had been painful for him. After some travels in Sicily, he went to Yugoslavia. In September 1963, several months after our departure from the U.S., when Fredy and I were looking for a European city to live in, we chose Belgrade, largely because of John's presence and his enthusiasm for the people and culture.

Fredy and I bought passage on a Swedish freighter which took us and our baggage to Copenhagen. We had earlier become friends with a Danish student of literature and we used his home in a Copenhagen suburb as a temporary stopping place before deciding on a more permanent location. We arrived in Denmark at the end of January 1963. We decided to wait for warmer weather before exploring other European cities, so after an initial stay with Poul Andreasen and his parents, we rented a furnished room in Gentofte, a short walk from our friend's home.

The three months we spent in these comfortable surroundings were a placid introduction to European life. We admired the efficient public transportation, the well-kept streets, the apparent social responsibility of the suburban Danes and the wonderful variety of salads and cakes for sale in the shops. We were an attentive audience for Poul's and his father's accounts of Danish resistance to Nazi occupation—a period less peaceful, for Denmark at least, than the early 1960s. The elder Andreasen had been in a concentration camp toward the end of the war.

During our three-month stay in Denmark, Fredy worked on his mid-twentieth century version of the Faust story. He never finished it, but the theme remained central to his conceptions. The two principal characters, Sabina and her father, were already clearly delineated in 1963. Each had a distinct attitude toward contemporary science. Fredy incorporated them as philosophical archetypes in *Letters of Insurgents*.

Cigarettes were very expensive in Denmark and Fredy tried pipe-smoking as a substitute for some of his cigarette consumption.

Efforts to learn Danish were moderately successful, although we never realized our goal of reading Ibsen in the original. To be sure they were available when we were ready for them, we bought his complete works before leaving Scandinavia.

The stay in Denmark ended on May 1, 1963. Helen and Tom Spiro, American friends who were in Europe on a Fulbright exchange, invited us to join them on a trip by car to Greece and Yugoslavia. We took camping gear which we used occasionally during the trip. In Zagreb we stayed with Yugoslav friends of the Spiros and in Belgrade stayed with John Ricklefs. We spent two weeks in Greece and saw many historical sites.

After a brief stay in Vienna, we went with the Spiros to Prague. Fredy was eager to visit the country of his birth. Our traveling companions had two acquaintances in Prague and we got in touch with them. Both spoke excellent English. The younger man was a thirty-year-old Party functionary who had studied in England and who assured us the Communist Parties, including the one in the U.S., provided an accurate analysis and an appropriate program for all who sought to improve social conditions in the world. When this man realized he was speaking to two such individuals, he advised us to return to the U.S. and become members of the Party. Fredy disputed the man's high opinion of the Party's qualities but realized that it was unlikely that this person would accept the viewpoint of a non-Party member. At the end of the conversation Fredy touchingly recited, in Czech, some poems and anthems he had learned as a child. The young administrator was undoubtedly baffled by this visitor.

The second man was less dogmatic and his advice was implicit, in the form of example, rather than explicit. He was a British intellectual who had emigrated to Czechoslovakia after World War II; during our conversation he told us his reasons for leaving England and about the post-war economic progress of his adopted country. He was no help, however, in furthering Fredy's request to stay in Prague as a student. Bureaucratic government officials immediately squelched any hopes of remaining in Czechoslovakia. The fact that Fredy had been born in Brno prompted suspicions rather than a welcome. I wonder if the two "non-official" men we contacted shared these suspicions. If so, they must have been impressed by our disguise: the Spiros having returned to Scandinavia, Fredy and I slept in a campground on the outskirts of the city and trudged around—often in the rain—looking a lot more like gypsies than conventional CIA employees.

The refusal of the Czech government to let us remain in Prague ruled out the only specific destination we had chosen for our new life in Europe. In mid-June 1963 we took an overnight train to Paris.

Having camped in our tent in Greece, Austria and Czechoslovakia, we immediately looked for a campground in or near Paris. And for several nights we slept in the Bois de Boulogne. Our living quarters became more comfortable when we moved our sleeping bag to the studio-loft of Eric Fischer, brother of our New York neighbor, Claire. Eric and his wife Myriam welcomed us to their city and milieu without reservation. We became acquainted with their friends and were often together.

At the beginning of July, Fredy and I moved to a fifth floor studio apartment (sublet for the summer) on rue St. Severin in the Latin Quarter and we enrolled at the Alliance Française. Until the end of August we immersed ourselves in French language and culture. With our friends, and even with each other, we spoke only French.

Eric encouraged us to see the films shown at the Cinémathèque and we became familiar with the "classics" of the cinema. We discussed theories of art with our painter and sculptor friends and took part in a new form of theater—a "happening" at the Au Bon Marché department store.

Political commitment took second place to cultural interests even though outraged chauvinism, an aftermath of the recent independence of Algeria, was agitating French political circles. In the 1960s, German tourists were visiting all parts of Western Europe and we sympathized with the grumbling French who resented them. It seemed unfair that the former occupiers could re-visit and bring their families to see places where, twenty years earlier, their authority had been imposed militarily. Few of the "victorious" French people could afford to travel abroad, and many Parisians had doubts about the assertion that Germany had lost the war.

The economic situation made it difficult for us to continue living in Paris. Wages were low compared to prices, and lodging was scarce and expensive. At the end of the summer we had two hundred dollars left and we knew it would not last long. We decided to go to Yugoslavia. Half our remaining money was spent on the trip from Paris to Belgrade; we rode with a Syrian worker who had spent the wages he had earned in France to buy a new car which he was driving to Damascus. The man had never learned to drive and even before leaving Paris, he had an accident that damaged his car. Fredy was the principal chauffeur during the three-day trip to Belgrade.

Six

Three Years in Yugoslavia

The warm welcome we received from numerous Yugoslavs in September 1963 made our move to Belgrade definitive. Within a few days we had found a room in the home of a bus driver and family on the outskirts of Zemun, a large suburb and extension of Belgrade on the other side of the Sava River. Fredy was hired for a temporary job as "speaker" by a media enterprise which made documentary films about tourist attractions in Yugoslavia. Fredy recorded the texts describing the sites depicted in the films: parks featuring post-war sculpture, monasteries, or coastal villages. For a few hours' work, he received the equivalent of U.S. wages and this money solved our immediate financial problems.

We enrolled at a language institute and spent every morning attending classes and listening to tapes of Serbo-Croatian. Our fellow students were from central Africa, Western Europe and the U.S.S.R. It was a friendly group and sometimes we got together outside of class. One of the two Soviet students was eager to meet for discussions but it was clear that the other disapproved of this extracurricular contact. We were shocked by Viktor's suspicious reserve and perhaps did not sufficiently appreciate Dimitri's courage in coming to visit us on his own.

The Yugoslav innovation of worker self-management was highly regarded in the West and we wanted to get acquainted with its principles and operation. Zemun had a number of factories and we had no trouble finding informed people to answer our questions. We quickly learned that Yugoslavs did not share the Western enthusiasm for worker self-management, considering it largely a public relations gimmick to camouflage conventional worker-vs.-management relations. We were surprised to learn that strikes were frequent. Although never reported in the press, the occurrence of this authentic worker-managed activity was common knowledge. Unions are an arm of the government (the "boss") so any strike in Yugoslavia necessarily occurs outside an institutional framework.

Even though we lived in their Zemun home for only two months, the Katić family introduced us to many Yugoslav customs and perspectives. The house was one of four or five units around a courtyard. Its design clearly originated in Serbian villages. There were no chickens in our courtyard, but we heard them in nearby enclosures. One outhouse served all the residents. As we had done in Paris, we went to public baths once or twice a week for showers.

When we moved into our room at the Katić's, our language skills in Serbian were almost non-existent. One of the neighbors, a toothless elderly man, took it upon himself to help us with vocabulary whenever he saw us; he would point to an object and name it. He taught us the numbers and was pleased with our progress. Unfortunately, the version of a word we learned from our toothless friend did not always correspond to the conventional pronunciation.

In addition to our language deficiencies, our working class hosts considered us backward in culinary skills. Local stores were quite unlike Danish and French ones and we sometimes were hard put to find ingredients for meals we knew how to prepare. We didn't know how to ask for meat in a butcher shop and were unfamiliar with outdoor markets, where most people in Zemun shopped. One day when we opened a can (of tuna, maybe), the entire Katić family stood around the table and watched. (The can opener was part of our camping gear; such a gadget would not have been found in their kitchen.) It wasn't that they had never seen canned goods, but they scorned unfresh food which came preserved in metal; nevertheless they were curious to see what emerged from the container and if we would eat it without further preparation. Once we became official students at the language institute we usually ate at student restaurants in Belgrade where we had a copious, if not a gourmet, midday meal.

During our three-year stay in Yugoslavia we ate extremely well. We found most of the Yugoslav dishes delicious. Two memorable meals were with the Katić family. One was on a Sunday in late September soon after our arrival. Mr. Katić had made it clear that we were invited to eat with them but we didn't know what the occasion was. We put on our Sunday clothes and waited. In late morning a large pig and a butcher arrived, and the afternoon was spent cutting up the carcass. A number of people took part—none of them wore Sunday clothes. They rendered lard, washed intestines for sausage casings, prepared the hams for smoking. In late afternoon we all sat down to a feast where pork liver was the principal dish.

Another Sunday we accompanied the Katić family and many of their friends and relatives to a wedding in a village about 75 miles from Zemun. Mr. Katić arranged for the use of a city bus of which he, naturally, was the driver. I can't remember if it was mechanical failure of the bus or if the road was in bad condition, but at one point the twenty or so wedding guests were obliged to get out of the bus and climb the hill; the men pushed the bus to the summit.

The wedding celebration consisted of eating, dancing and drinking. The ceremony itself must have preceded or followed the afternoon events. We ate outside, at long tables; roast pig—the highlight of the meal—was prepared over an open fire. Fredy, who never liked meat, was more appreciative of the *gibanica* (a pasta and cheese dish) and other delicacies than of the roast pork.

Music was provided by local musicians who, as the festivities continued, received generous donations, usually in the form of bills which were affixed to their foreheads (and which sweat kept there until the end of the piece). The dances were line dances and men, women and children of all ages took part, even Fredy and I. The elderly executed every step and turn, but in miniature, so to speak. They hardly raised their foot off the ground, twisted their torso only slightly, reserving their strength. But the rhythm was flawless and every nuance observed. We had been told that dances give an opportunity for young women to display their endurance and for village bachelors to judge the vigor of potential brides. I hope the dances served a less crass function, but, it's true, the bride (although already chosen) danced exuberantly from beginning to end. And she was not the only unflagging woman dancer among the celebrants.

In Belgrade, young people had other, less exhausting, criteria when seeking a spouse. Getting acquainted often took place in a well-defined downtown area during the afternoon promenade. On a street (closed to vehicles) leading from Terazija to Kalemegdan Park, one saw crowds of people every afternoon.

At all hours of the day there were also crowds of people at the train station—most of them were coming to the city to live. Fredy observed that we were seeing the migration from the countryside to the city. Zemun was hardly the countryside, but in November we joined the influx to Belgrade, taking a room in an apartment with modern conveniences. Fredy enrolled as a graduate student at the Economics Faculty and I found two jobs in music--one playing, one teaching.

It was our responsibility to secure a visa; since our situation had few precedents, various authorities quoted widely divergent rules. The bureaucrat in one office assured us we had to return to the United States and apply for a visa from there. After trying to communicate the absurdity of this proposal, we left and continued our search at another office which, conveniently, was nearby. Here we were immediately given one-year visas. We wondered if this was the Yugoslav self-managed economy at work.

Most of our Yugoslav friends and associates had been born and raised in Belgrade, but almost all of them had relatives who still lived in villages. The rural ties were part of our friends' self-definition. Fredy and I were often invited to go with them to visit their parents, grandparents or aunts and uncles. In the course of numerous visits, we traveled to villages that had no roads connecting them; we had a view of Spring as a season of mud; we slept on straw mattresses and helped shell corn by hand. The meals served us were always delicious (sometimes an animal was slaughtered in honor of our visit). It was obvious that our peasant hosts worked long hours doing by hand heavy tasks that a machine could accomplish in a fraction of the time, and it puzzled us that there was not more interest in labor-saving techniques. Though acknowledging that both men and women took great pride in their work, Fredy judged peasant life to be difficult and unrewarding.

As a student of economics, concerned with flow charts which showed the transfer of goods on a national level, Fredy had a patronizing view of the average peasant's undertaking. The efforts they expended and the time it took (which they never "counted") to bring their products to city markets made him scornful of their form of distribution and exchange. We were not well informed about collectivization efforts, but when he saw peasants hoeing in the long "ribbon" fields on which tractors would have been very efficient, Fredy felt justified in criticizing the peasants' reluctance to relinquish control over their private plots.

His later studies of Kosovo and Metohija (Kosmet)* softened this view somewhat and he became more sympathetic to peasants who

---

*An autonomous region within Serbia whose capital is Priština. The majority of Kosmet's inhabitants are Albanian who retain tribal bonds, speak their own language and practice the Muslim religion.

resisted plans imposed by bureaucrats. In the summer of 1965, Fredy went with a friend and fellow student, Velimir Morača, to visit the latter's family and village in Montenegro. His stay there impressed him. First because of the isolation: the walk from the train station was ten miles, uphill. Then by the self-sufficiency of these peasant-herders: the only thing they bought was salt. Finally, by the fierce independence: Morača's uncle refused to use a plate when eating, even though there were guests from the city. Fredy quoted this man's vigorous rejection of modern utensils: "Horse shit! What do I need a goddam fucking plate for?"

Urban Yugoslavs, too, were free with their criticisms, although they generally were not too specific, at least in public, when it came to government policies and individuals. Dissidents ran a very real risk of becoming political prisoners. Morača, who became close friends with Fredy, had spent eight years in jail because of his beliefs. People often explained to us that backwardness and social problems were due to "the three hundred years the Serbs lived under the Turkish yoke." Another semi-serious explanation for the country's difficulties was presented in the form of a frequently quoted joke: Question: "Who invented scientific socialism?" Response: "Marx and Engels." Comment: "Shouldn't they have tried it on rats first?" Newspapers rarely attacked official policies but did criticize certain aspects of them and often printed indignant letters from readers. At the theater we heard more profound, albeit more abstract, critiques. Few of our Yugoslav acquaintances hesitated to criticize the government, but all were wary of the authorities' power.

Fredy's only critique which reached the mass media was a letter he wrote to the Belgrade papers expressing his indignation at finding a nail in a package of dry soup mix. By then he was familiar with the conventional clichés used to praise Yugoslav socialism and he used them to good effect.

Neither Turkish occupation nor socialism were cited as sources for Yugoslav notions of male supremacy; it presumably had more indigenous roots. Fredy, always sensitive to the practice and verbalization of discrimination, observed that although Yugoslav men vigorously defended male prerogatives, they accepted a large share of domestic responsibility, especially if they had a wife who worked outside the home. Fredy pointed out this gap between principles and practice to some of his male friends. They explained that the situation in *their* home was different, that *their* wife needed assistance, still insisting that the tasks of marketing, child-rearing, cooking and cleaning really were a woman's obligation. A few years later, in texts written in Kalamazoo, Fredy examined other gaps between ideology and practice. One of these was the example of workers who, while verbally denouncing rebellious actions in one breath, take drastic, vigorous steps to protect their own interests in the next. Another example furnished a theme that remained central to all his later writings (in this case, admirable principles are belied by reprehensible practice): the political agitator whose goal is freedom, but who, once in power (and sometimes even before), justifies coercion in the name of a higher good.

Before the end of his first year in Belgrade, Fredy already spoke fluent Serbian and was able to read the textbooks for his classes. In the two subsequent years he learned to speak even better, although never without grammatical faults. People from certain regions in Yugoslavia ignore rules of declension, and new acquaintances often assumed that Fredy was from one of those regions.

To each other we spoke English, however, and some of our friends were English-speaking. Once or twice a month we read plays with John Ricklefs, Paul Pignon (who worked in Belgrade as a technical translator and who composed music when not working), Paul's wife Jasna and an Australian woman (who was spending a year in Belgrade to get acquainted with the country her parents had left).

We had many opportunities to attend excellent concerts of world-famous artists (Kogan, Richter, Ricci) and Fredy heard many of the opera performances in which I participated as an orchestra violinist.

One of Fredy's undertakings which remained unfinished was a translation into English of a history of Serbia. He worked on this project with a friend; I think that too much time of the weekly sessions was spent on eating and discussing and too little on translating.

Between 1963 and 1966, we did some traveling outside Yugoslavia. In the summer of 1964, we spent five weeks in Italy, visiting Venice, Ravenna, Rome, Naples and Florence. In 1965 when the Belgrade Opera made a tour of East Germany, Fredy traveled with the company; we spent a week in both East Berlin and Leipzig. He and I made independent visits, mostly short, to Budapest, Sofia and Bucharest. In the summer of 1965 when I went to the U.S., Fredy traveled in Yugoslavia; in Sarajevo he had a brief reunion with Living Theatre friends (who were performing throughout Europe that year). He also went to Paris to renew friendships there.

For most of the stay in Belgrade, Fredy devoted himself to his studies and was a conscientious student. At the Economics Faculty at least two of his professors were high in governmental circles. One was president of the national bank; he came to class in a chauffeur-driven Mercedes. The other was the wife of the country's vice-president. Both professors appear in *Letters of Insurgents.*

In his first year of study, Fredy took courses which presented Marxist principles of economic analysis and which used this analysis to study the Yugoslav economy. In the second year the courses were more specialized. Two foreign professors came to lecture: one, a Hungarian mathematician, taught the students how to construct and use input-output matrices; the other, a Soviet economist, discussed the latest management techniques. The textbooks for both classes were by U.S. academics.*

Fredy's master's thesis, "The Structure of Backwardness," which he completed in the spring of 1965 was a statistical-economic analysis of certain factors in a number of countries at various levels of industrial development. He used flow charts to study consumption, exports and reinvestment in five basic sectors. In no way does this work foreshadow Fredy's later, critical, views on industrialization. One of its assumptions is "that a developed economy is a backward economy's image of the future. . . There may be various 'roads to socialism,' but there is only one road to industrialization: it is a broad highway which may be followed in the freshness of April or the heat of August; one may walk it, ride a horse or go by bulldozer; if he cannot follow it he will not get where it leads" (page 97). The destination itself goes unquestioned in this work.

The panel of professors to whom he presented his thesis was satisfied with its quality even though, at the public defense, some of them quibbled about certain of Fredy's observations about Yugoslavia. The academic panel's chief, wife of the country's vice-president, commented on Comrade Perlman's remarkable fluency in Serbian.

Fredy found the bland, "official" analyses offered by the Economics Faculty less and less interesting and was pleased to follow courses of and get acquainted with Miloš Samardžija, economics professor at the Law Faculty. This former consultant to the national

*The use of American textbooks did not upset Fredy when he took these courses. But after returning to the U.S. where he met Western partisans of scientific socialism who insisted that Soviet economic principles and practices were superior to those in the West, Fredy cited his Yugoslav experience to counter their claims. Fredy maintained that contemporary scientific socialists unreservedly advocate American management principles.

government had a profound knowledge of Marx and Marxist theoreticians, and was an unequivocal proponent of industrialization. He did not question the goals of the Yugoslav government, but his pragmatic observations combined with his discerning Marxist perspective resulted in trenchant critiques of the Yugoslav system.

The doctoral thesis which Fredy presented to the Law Faculty where Samardžija was his advisor, was more controversial than the earlier thesis. In this one, Fredy attacked specific economic practices of the Yugoslav government, investment decisions which related to Kosmet.* He used Preobrazhensky's analysis of the primitive accumulation of capital to study prospects for Kosmet's development and concluded that the other Yugoslav republics should build industrial plants in Kosmet. Failure to do this would heighten the backwardness. Fredy worked hard on this study and gathered much material to defend his conclusions: a statistical study of Yugoslav per capita income since 1945; a documentation of the transfer of the labor force from agriculture; intersectoral comparisons between republics. He thought that the proposals he made were reasonable, that the data he had assembled and carefully analyzed with modern mathematical methods should convince rational people interested in the economic development of all parts of the country. He was disturbed by the warning he got from the more worldly-wise Samardžija not to dwell on the implications of his thesis when he defended it in front of the other professors. Samardžija suggested that these men did not welcome dissertations – no matter how well documented and how closely argued – whose conclusions called on the country's leaders to change their policies. In June 1966 Fredy defended his "Conditions for the Development of a Backward Region" and was awarded a Ph.D. from the Belgrade University Law Faculty.

During his last year in Belgrade, while still a student at the Law Faculty, Fredy was also a member of an economic planning commission hired by the regional administration in Kosmet. The task of the commission was to propose a program for development. Samardžija was head of this commission; other Law Faculty graduate students also participated. Fredy made many trips to Priština but he did not get a close view of daily life in the region nor did he get acquainted with non-administrative Albanian residents, since most of his time in Priština was spent in offices.

*See note on page 35.

Fredy found this "job" (for which he was well paid) interesting but not particularly satisfying. He realized that the commission was concerned mainly with words, abstractions, and that the situation of Kosmet's population did not change as a result of his and his colleagues' proposals. A few years later Fredy would criticize the legitimacy of planning commissions as such.

Most of Fredy's fellow students were preparing for a career in the Yugoslav bureaucracy and had little interest in initiating changes in economic policies. One friend (who was not a participant in the Kosmet commission) was already employed by a Novi Sad enterprise; he had pursued graduate studies at the request of his superiors. Six months after his graduation we visited Miša in his new office. Except for the handsome furniture surrounding our friend, the room was empty. As we drank the Turkish coffee brought to us by the woman hired by the enterprise to make and serve coffee, we asked Miša to tell us about his job responsibilities. With only a trace of sheepishness, he explained that as yet his duties were undefined; he assured us, however, that before the end of the year the enterprise directors would undoubtedly assign him some projects. When we left, he took the newspaper from a desk drawer and resumed his on-the-job activity.

The experiences of Velimir Morača gave us a more somber view of Yugoslav reality. Although at least one of his close relatives was a famous World War II partisan, the young Morača's views concerning Yugoslavia's break with the Soviet Union (in 1948) brought him prison sentences totaling eight years. During his incarceration, he read all of Marx's and Lenin's works and exercised his photographic memory on these and other texts. In the mid-1960s Morača was out of prison. He lived and worked in Subotica, but commuted to Belgrade to study at the Economics Faculty.

This ex-political prisoner who was trying to understand the society in which he lived was the model Fredy took for Yarostan in *Letters of Insurgents*. The disorientation Yarostan described in his letters to Sophia was all too familiar to Morača. The experiences of Yarostan's daughter Vesna closely follow the history of Morača's daughter of the same name. This intelligent and patriotic ten-year-old was confused by the ambiguous position of her father: what could he have done to warrant his being jailed by the authorities of a country based on such admirable principles? The real Vesna's death occurred after we had left Yugoslavia so Fredy's depiction of her death in *Letters* was hypothetical. Morača himself was rearrested in the 1970s and died in prison. This friend's history — especially the tragic events which occurred after we left the country — played a great part in determining Fredy's over-all estimation of the Yugoslav system. Morača's uncompromising nature, his commitment to economic equality and his outspoken critiques were intolerable to the authorities. With absolute clarity, Fredy saw in Morača the individual destroyed by the State.

Our departure from Yugoslavia in 1966 was rather precipitous, but not related to political repression. Yugoslav doctors advised me to return to the United States following an illness and surgery. Had I not been ill, it is likely we would have remained another year in Belgrade. But contestations and anti-war actions made the U.S. seem more interesting than it had four years earlier, and it is probable that we would have returned soon after Fredy finished his studies at the University of Belgrade. We had been welcomed and appreciated in Belgrade and when, after a three-year stay, we bid farewell to our friends, activities, the city itself, we already felt nostalgia and loss.

Seven

A Short Career in Academia

A recommendation by Samardžija resulted in Fredy's being offered a two-year appointment as assistant professor at Western Michigan University in Kalamazoo, Michigan. Samardžija himself was visiting professor in the Economics Department at the university in 1966-67. A small city in mid-America was not our first choice among places to live but this job had the advantage of solving financial problems. The return to American surroundings — the pervasive and huge automobiles, the vast supermarkets, the well-tended lawns encircling gadget-filled homes — required a period of adaptation. In this time of aggressive war, the naive joviality of the population and its passion to consume disturbed and offended Fredy.

In the first two years in Kalamazoo, Fredy was not a fringe person. Although constantly involved in controversies, he spoke as an intellectual attached to an institution of higher learning and as a knowledgeable analyst of the Yugoslav economy and culture. The first essay he wrote after returning to the U.S. was a critique of the way social science was taught in American universities. He even traveled to an academic gathering to read it, and the essay was published in a journal of education. In "Critical Education" Fredy identified three types of educators: traditional, adaptive and critical. Capitalist society needs critical thinkers in science and technology, and educators in these field teach students to question their predecessors' assumptions. But in the social sciences, current education discourages students from questioning underlying assumptions. Fredy called for the critical perspective to be applied to these fields as well.

He even furnished a technique for achieving this end: By studying social critics of an earlier epoch, a student can "play-act" the role of critic and thus prepare himself or herself for a similar role in contemporary society.

This was, in fact, the approach Fredy took in the classes he taught, nearly all of which were introductions to social science. Fredy was an outspoken opponent of U.S. involvement in Vietnam but in his lectures tried to show his students what brought him to this position rather than trying to convert his listeners by authority. He was generous with his time and willing to overlook sometimes shocking deficiencies in the students' knowledge of history and geography; but he was intolerant of the fervent confidence in American superiority expressed by some of the young people. He expected students to call him by his first name and in his second year he let them give themselves the grades they wanted.

In a second essay, "Corporate-Military Culture and the Social Sciences," Fredy expanded arguments presented in "Critical Education." Quoting with approval Veblen's assertion about machine industry needing a socialist organization of society to function at its best, Fredy maintained that contemporary governments and corporations try to inhibit the "subversive, iconoclastic patterns of thought which accompanied the development of technology." The essay, never published, ends with a proposal for student-run courses in which speakers invited by the students would address the class.

Fredy was himself a serious student while in Kalamazoo. He took a course in Russian; he read carefully all of Marx's works, reread the classical economists and familiarized himself with American social science, especially Thorstein Veblen and Leslie White. Fredy deplored the widespread use of Paul Samuelson's textbook on economics, and insisted that the economic principles propounded by Samuelson reduced economic theory to simplistic formulas which ignored reality. In an essay on Ricardo and Preobrazhensky Fredy contrasted the works of these two economists with that of the Panglossian dean of American economic theory.

In 1967, Fredy and Samardžija translated I.I. Rubin's *Essays on Marx's Theory of Value* from Russian, via Samardžija's Serbo-Croatian, into English. Fredy's "Essay on Commodity Fetishism," written the following year, served as an introduction to Rubin's book when we published the translation in 1971. The "Essay" was also printed separately in Argentina, Italy and the U.S. In this work Fredy examines Marx's theory of alienation in capitalist society, citing Marx for his point of departure: "As individuals express their life, so they are. What they are, therefore, coincides with their production, both in *what* they produce and with *how* they produce." Fredy also pursued his critique of American mainstream economics, distinguishing Marx's concerns from those of Samuelson: "Marx constructs a model of 'a simple commodity economy' . . . in order to learn how labor is regulated in an economy where this regulation takes place through the exchange of things."

If Marx and Veblen gave Fredy theoretical insights about American society, the Western Michigan University faculty members' ostracism of his friend and colleague, Bob Rafferty, provided a first-hand view of witch-hunting in practice. Rafferty maintained that most people don't see—don't even want to see--the reality that surrounds them. When an astronaut first "walked" on the moon, Rafferty asserted that this man was no explorer and, as an extension of a machine, could have had no human response to what he had been programmed to see. Mediated experience had merely reached a higher level of perfection.

Rafferty usually aimed his critiques at persons closer at hand, and excelled at exposing ugly sentiments lurking behind the liberal phrases of his fellow professors. The Vietnam war was making people take sides and most faculty members referred to the U.S. military forces in southeast Asia as "We." Rafferty brought out the racism implicit in their incredulity that non-white peasants could defeat the sophisticated white men and their weapons.

In these days when Solzhenitsyn was documenting conformity and resistance elsewhere, Rafferty exposed the sensible Kalamazoo professors as toadies of the U.S. system. Unfortunately the number of people who recognized his acuity and skill was small. The professors in the Economics Department of Western Michigan University—conventional in both thought and lifestyle—were not grateful for his insights. Rafferty, as he himself had told them on numerous occasions, was not like them; so these insecure men had no misgivings about terminating their outspoken colleague's connection with their school. In the months between their decision and the end of the academic year, these faculty members treated Rafferty with contempt. This meant his forum was limited mainly to the classroom; his isolation made him yet more abrasive and outrageous. It was common for him to open his lectures to the undergraduate students with the assertion that "the U.S. army is getting its pants licked off in Vietnam." Sometimes his analysis lost touch with reality as when, for example, he confidently spoke of the not-far-off day when the Soviet navy would sail triumphantly into the Great Lakes.

Fredy remembered "Jenny's Song" from *The Three Penny Opera* and observed that Bertold Brecht must have known someone like Rafferty. Contemptuous of the system's apologists, but unable to see himself outside the university, Rafferty was frustrated and hurt by his exclusion. Brecht lets the outcast Jenny flaunt her ultimate victory and savor the revenge she will inflict on her humiliators. During the politically bleak days of 1967, Rafferty shared Jenny's unforgiving rage.

> . . .you still have no idea who I may be,
> But one evening there'll be a roar down by the harbor
> And you'll ask: what's the reason for that roar?
> And you'll see me standing staring through the window
> And you'll ask: now what's she grinning for?
> > And the ship with eight sails
> > And with fifty great cannon
> > Will start shooting the town.
>
> . . . .
> And at midday you will see a hundred men come ashore
> Who will search the shadows so still now.
> And they'll capture every single living person they can see
> And put them in chains and bring them to me
> And ask: which of these shall we kill now?
> And when the sun stands at noon there'll be a hush down by
> the harbor
> As they ask me which of these are doomed to die
> And then you'll hear me saying to them: All o' them!
> And when their heads fall, I shall shout: Hoppla!
> > And the ship with eight sails
> > And with fifty great cannon
> > Will sail homewards with me.*

In the fluorescent-lit corridors and formica-filled offices of small-minded men who pretended this locale was a Socratic forum, Rafferty became a non-person. The exclusion of his office-mate turned Fredy's initial amiability toward other faculty members into antagonistic disdain. He realized that when they defended professors who did military research, they were defending their own interests and that almost

*Translated by Eric Bentley, in *From the Modern Repertoire, Series One,* Bloomington, 1955, pp. 241-2.

all of them longed to be hired as economic consultants to the air force or to the local drug corporation, Upjohn. Before leaving Kalamazoo, Fredy's own dislike for the American university and its functionaries appeared in a vitriolic essay he entitled, "I Accuse this Liberal University of Terror and Violence." His friend Bob Rafferty had furnished him with several of the arguments.

In early 1968, for his final semester at Western Michigan University, Fredy arranged to be "advisor" to a student-run course like the one he had proposed in his essay, "Corporate-Military Culture and the Social Sciences." This experiment was not an unqualified success but gave him a chance to test his assumptions about American education. It was expecting a great deal from the young students in Kalamazoo to choose topics, carry out research and present their conclusions to others. Given the inexperience of nearly everyone in the class, the successful sessions were all the more remarkable. The diligent efforts of three or four of the student-participants made Fredy feel his pedagogical theories were correct, but he recognized that passivity had already been inculcated in most of the students and that a few months of a student-run course were not likely to change deeply ingrained habits.

At the end of the last session, Fredy came to the front of the lecture hall. After a few remarks about the class itself, he publicly presented a gold ring along with a challenge to one of the students, a well-read, articulate intellectual who was committed to social change. The ring, which Fredy had worn for three years, had come from an Angolan revolutionary; it had come to Fredy from its previous wearer, a Yugoslav dissident living in Paris. Sharing the ring was to foster a commitment to fight injustice and create a bond of solidarity between those who had worn it. Fredy's challenge, which accompanied the ring, called for purposeful, principled action outside the classroom. The ceremony was, in fact, Fredy's last appearance in an American classroom.

He did, however, lecture in Italian classrooms for a few weeks in the spring of both 1968 and 1969. The state-subsidized Institut universitaire d'études Européennes in Turin, Italy offered a non-degree program for students from North America, Europe and Africa. The three-week course that Fredy gave in 1968 was on economic theories and techniques; he lectured in French.

When the course in Turin ended, Fredy took a train to Paris and found himself caught up in the tumultuous events of May 1968. His experiences during these intense, joyous weeks deeply affected his views and remained a constant reference point whenever he considered possibilities for social change. It was immediately clear that the upheaval was not taking the form Jenny or Rafferty had anticipated. Neither a firing squad with orders to "Kill them all!" nor the appearance of the Soviet navy in the Great Lakes were possible outcomes of the rebellion in Paris in May 1968.

The act of rebellion itself was exhilarating. The massive street actions in which thousands confronted the forces of the status quo gave rise to hopes that the old world was about to be overturned. Within days, the prestige of political parties, representatives and experts, melted. Many buildings were occupied, and the State's authority was effectively excluded from these liberated areas. People organized committees to carry out necessary tasks. There was a feverish exchange of views, proposals for collective activity. Discussions went on around the clock — some in an amphitheater where there was a microphone, but mostly between individuals who were discovering the joys that the mass media had deprived them of. There was a widespread conviction that one's daily activity was about to be transformed and that everyone would participate in choosing and bringing about new social arrangements.

Fredy took part in a loosely-organized group of intellectuals, students and young workers who held discussions at the Censier classroom complex and who also tried to communicate their aspirations to auto workers who lived and worked in the Paris suburbs. The Communist Party labor union, the CGT, did not welcome the enthusiastic agitators who came to initiate dialogue with the striking workers for whom it claimed to speak. Union officials feared that they could lose control over "their" strike if the workers insisted on changing the demands from the usual ones concerned with wages to ones which the union could not easily co-opt. Therefore, they kept the factory gates locked and insisted on mediating all contacts with the workers who were occupying the factory. The union bureaucrats finally agreed to transmit an appeal by the "outsiders" to the workers, and one union functionary, using a microphone, gave a distorted account of who the militants were and why they had come to this factory. Since many of the assembled workers were non-French, the outside agitators insisted that the appeal should be presented in Spanish and Serbo-Croatian as well. The union officials grudgingly agreed, and gave the microphone to Fredy who was delighted to convey the actual appeal.

On another occasion, when a group of Censier activists went to talk to workers at a suburban factory, a number of them were arrested for trespassing. They had climbed over the factory fence, attempting to speak to the workers directly. At the arraignment Fredy explained to the judge that he was an American professor and that he had climbed the fence in order to carry out research about French labor unions. The judge was undoubtedly skeptical, but charges against Fredy were dropped.

Many of the mass demonstrations in Paris ended with the construction of barricades and confrontations with the police. Tear gas was frequently used and demonstrators were chased and beaten by aggressive riot squad police. Though he was never beaten, Fredy fell ill after one demonstration and spent two days in bed, unconscious most of the time.

During these action-filled weeks, there was little time for reading, but Fredy learned about ideas and histories which influenced him in the decade which followed: the texts of the Situationist International, anarchism and the Spanish Revolution, the council communists.

In July 1968, as law and order were being reimposed on French society, Fredy returned to the United States, stopping briefly in New York City to meet and exchange views with militants involved in the student strike and building occupation at Columbia University.

At the end of August, Fredy was again protesting in the streets — this time in Chicago at the Democratic Party convention. Tear gas was widely used here too. The brutality of the Chicago cops was intimidating, but we interpreted their response as proof that our disruptions were communicating a rejection of the government's policies.

In Chicago we met dissidents from all parts of the U.S. A number of friendships were begun during these days, especially with anarchist and IWW* militants who resided in Chicago. We visited SDS† centers, admired their printing facilities and talked to people who would soon become Weathermen. We also attended workshops organized by the New University Movement whose concerns were largely restricted to university reform.

Several of these new acquaintances visited us in Kalamazoo in subsequent months. The anticipation of imminent change the visitors brought with them was more remarkable than our intellectual exchanges with them. The sense that the itinerant militants were central

*Industrial Workers of the World
†Students for a Democratic Society

actors in a movement that would fundamentally transform American society was enhanced by the presence of secret service agents who followed them around Kalamazoo.

In the late 1960s agitation centered mainly around the war in Vietnam, but the ubiquitous American racism was also being challenged. Riots in Detroit in 1967 had disrupted factory and civic life, and confrontations continued there and elsewhere in Michigan. In Kalamazoo, the Black Action Movement had articulate spokesmen; their occupation of the university administration building following the assassination of Martin Luther King, Jr. made us respect their courage and conviction.

Militants from Europe also visited us in Kalamazoo. One of them, Roger Gregoire, stayed with us for several months, working with Fredy on an account and evaluation of experiences the two had shared in May and June 1968 while members of the Citroën Worker-Student Action Committee. The resulting 96-page history and analysis was printed in the spring of 1969. Roger also participated in and observed local actions; and he furnished printing skills for some numbers of the *Black & Red* periodical which had been launched in September 1968.

Many other people collaborated on the six issues of Kalamazoo *Black & Red*. All were students at Western Michigan University; for at least three of them, Linda Lanphear, Bob Maier and a German exchange student, non-academic activities took precedence over their studies. In addition to the creative efforts connected with writing, typing and printing the 70-page monthly publication, there were frequent interventions in classes, a student strike, SDS meetings, reprisals by faculty members and, naturally, long discussions about implications of these actions and responses. During the 1968-69 academic year Fredy had no official ties with the university.

Printing equipment was not available to us in Kalamazoo, but we did find a printer willing to make negatives of the typewritten copy which had been prepared on a portable Hermes machine and laid out using a makeshift light-box. When we had everything ready to print, we went to Ann Arbor to use the facilities of the Radical Education Project (REP), an SDS printing collective.

After they had showed us how to use the equipment, the REP staff treated us as equals and gave us free access to the space. We paid them for the materials we used, helped them with collating or with other menial tasks and left things clean when finished. REP's openness greatly impressed Fredy, all the more since it was clear

to everyone that the texts we were printing did not at all conform
to the political perspective of the Ann Arbor collective. He considered
this collaboration with REP to be mutually rewarding and often cited
it as a model of cooperative activity.

Fredy found the gap between theory and practice in Kalamazoo
activist circles to be as disappointing as the relationship with the REP
staff was encouraging. Marx's observation which ridicules the no-
tion that ideas can change the world (an observation Fredy often
quoted), provided a relevant – and severe – critique of many gran-
diose proposals put forward in SDS planning sessions during the
autumn of 1968. Students who were unable to compose, print or
distribute either a leaflet or a poster, nevertheless did not hesitate
to visualize the proposed strike at the university spreading to all of
Kalamazoo and encompassing Michigan and the entire country. A
humorous but devastating parody of this "fantastic" approach to revolution was made in *Black & Red Number 4:* "We Called a Strike and
No One Came." And insights gained from discussions with people
advocating unrealizable projects while continuing to accept the everyday humiliations and obligations imposed by capitalist society became
part of *The Reproduction of Daily Life* which Fredy wrote during
his last winter in Kalamazoo.

This 24-page pamphlet is Fredy's most widely read work. We
printed and distributed several thousand copies and it has been
translated into French, Portuguese and Swedish. The essay gives a
concise exposition of Marx's analysis of commodity fetishism; in this
context Fredy ridicules the "holy trinity" invoked by Western economic
theory to describe production and exchange: Land, Labor and Capital.
Capital, the "obvious hero of the piece," is seen in another light after
Fredy examines it: Capital is neither a natural force nor a man-made
monster; its power does not "reside in the material receptacles in which
the labor of past generations is stored." Nor does the power of Capital
"reside in money, since money is a social convention which has no
more 'power' than men are willing to grant it; when men refuse to
sell their labor, money cannot perform even the simplest tasks, because
money does not 'work.' " Nevertheless, Capital's abstract but uncanny
power drastically changes society in all corners of the world:

> Independent as well as dependent hunters, peasants and crafts-
> men, free men as well as slaves, are transformed into hired
> laborers. . . [T]hose who were previously conscious creators of

their own meager existence become unconscious victims of their own activity even while abolishing the meagerness of their existence. Men who were much but had little now have much but are little. [pp. 21-24]

Between September 1968 and April 1969, six issues of *Black & Red* were produced. They provided information about resistance and rebellion in the United States and Europe and also offered texts of the Situationist International as well as analyses of contemporary society, focusing especially on Kalamazoo and Western Michigan University. Fredy's essay "Anything Can Happen," which appeared in the first issue, asserted that assumptions about the common sense and passivity of people in France, the U.S. and elsewhere had been shown to have been false, as was the social scientists' perception of everyone being conventional and liking it.

Black & Red Number 2 was devoted mainly to events in Chicago during the Democratic Party convention. Clever and satirical Yippie actions like nominating a pig for president were contrasted with the grim violence of the police and their supervisors. In one article Fredy pointed out that after the forces of law and order attacked certain white Americans on the streets of Chicago, the victims revised their view of institutional defenders of freedom.

For years the press has reported the poisoning, maiming and murder of "Vietcong terrorists," "peasant guerrillas," Black "snipers" and "looters," with the same cool indifference that one would use to describe the extermination of insects. The reader was always made to understand that "our boys" did what they did for the sake of "freedom" and to maintain "law and order."

However, when the press was attacked, gassed and beaten by "our boys," the Chicago cops, adjectives like "vicious," "sadistic," "violent," and "cruel" were used in the finest papers of the country, not to describe "terrorists" but to describe "our boys," the agents of "law and order." [p. 43]

A challenge to white radicals by the Kalamazoo Black Action Movement opened *Black & Red Number 3.* It was followed by a lengthy self-critique of actions initiated on the Western Michigan University campus by the Committee on Higher Education (CHE). There was also an account of the Belgrade "students' insurrection" in June 1968 and a first installment of the Situationist International's "The Poverty of Student Life."

Issue Number 4 was devoted almost entirely to "We Called a Strike and No One Came." It appeared in the form of a collage of famous European paintings and bubbles which contained succinct presentations of the various outlooks held by SDS members who were calling on Western Michigan University students to strike on November 5, 1968. Fredy's most vivid memory of the meeting where strategies were discussed was of the stomach ache he was suffering from. On page 34, Fredy's criticisms of proposals are interspersed with groans about his discomfort—all coming from the mouth of an angel.

Illustrations with bubbles continued in issue Number 5. Here, the medium was used to expose the capitalist university; the text juxtaposed the ideological obfuscation (taken from the Western Michigan University official publications) and the actual goals of domestication which the educational process aims for. The issue concludes with "The Fetish Speaks," a compilation of Marx's quotes "spoken" by a variety of commodities.

Black & Red Number 6 contains reprints of documents and posters from the November 1968 strike at Western Michigan University. Among them is "Initiation Rites for Students," a more succinct presentation of the exposure in *Black & Red Number 5*. This two-sided flyer was subsequently reprinted and diffused in many other cities and countries. Fredy's indignant evaluation of the university, "I Accuse this Liberal University of Terror and Violence," was also printed in this issue. In it Fredy rails at his former colleagues:

> Liberals are not "moderate." That's their own self-image. They're extremists, but unlike reactionaries, THEY'RE EX-TREMISTS WITH GOOD CONSCIENCES. Their instruments are not "ideas"; their instruments are TERROR and VIOLENCE. But unlike lynchers, THE LIBERALS TURN THEIR EYES AWAY to maintain their innocence. [p. 53]

In April 1969, three weeks after *Black & Red Number 6* was printed, Fredy left Kalamazoo and thereafter rarely concerned himself with the university or the bad faith of its liberal professors. He never changed his mind about the role that this institution serves. Even though he was often enthusiastic about works of scholars who held academic posts, he did not revise his judgment about the establishments they were affiliated with.

Fredy's attitude toward academia was clarified by the evaluation he made of his former professor, C. Wright Mills. A 110-page essay, completed in April 1969, resulted from Fredy's examination of Mills' search for an agency to bring about social change. Fredy viewed this search as the only proper subject matter for sociological inquiry and he interpreted Mills' work in the light of this effort. The subtitle of the essay is *C. Wright Mills' Struggle to Unite Knowledge and Action;* the title, *The Incoherence of the Intellectual,* suggests how Fredy judged Mills' success.

Fredy argues that Mills was led away from his search by the constraints of the academic establishment. Fredy particularly disapproves of the collaboration with Professor Hans Gerth. Mills is depicted as a "masterless, recalcitrant man, at times almost a sort of intellectual Wobbly" (p. 60), who started with a singularly coherent perspective with which to judge "the cheerful robot, the technological idiot, the crackpot realist" (p. 76). The perspective that Fredy claims was clouded by sociology's constrictive discipline had been furnished to some extent by Veblen's insights and by Mills' own appreciation of "the ethos of craftsmanship...as the central experience of the unalienated human being and the very root of free human development" (pp. 76-77).

Although he admired the Wobblies, Mills did not see organized labor as a likely agency for social change. One of his early books documented the extent to which labor leaders functioned as cogs in the restrictive social mechanism. Mills held out some hope for the critical, committed intellectual if he or she could begin to ask fundamental questions about urgent social concerns and abandon efforts to solve problems defined by the ruling class. In Fredy's words:

> What Mills prophetically called for was a confrontation between idiocy and coherence, a showdown between the fully developed human being and the cheerful robot, technological idiot, a destruction of the rationality without reason...
> Mills lucidly defined a large goal, and shortly after his premature death a new left began to take concrete steps toward its realization in every region of the world; even a new American left began to move upstream against the main drift. However, in order to define the available courses of action and the obstacles on the way, Mills himself had to struggle against the frenzy and trash and fraud which had been stuffed into his mind and file by academic bureaucrats and their hired and scared

satraps. In this struggle, he had to spend vast amounts of energy
to reach a level of coherence and clarity which he had already
reached in 1948. [p. 81]

    Fredy noted that Mills, near the end of his life, was looking
beyond the academy, seeking what he called "genuine alternatives."
Fredy was disappointed that Mills, in his reading of Marx, seemed
to miss an essential aspect of the analysis, and he reproaches Mills
for reducing alienation to "psychic exploitation," the question of the
attitude of men toward the work they do.

> Since Mills does not regard the alienation of people's self-powers
> as a daily activity but as a *psychic* condition, he cannot regard
> the de-alienation of these powers as revolutionary activity but
> merely as another *psychic* condition. All that can change is the
> institutional form of alienation, the type of bureaucratic *orders*
> within which people perform their *roles*. [p. 113]

    It was Mills' "struggle to unite knowledge and action" that led
Fredy to identify closely with the man. He had gained enormously
both from Mills' social analysis and from examining the differences
between them. Fredy was determined to avoid the deadends that had
frustrated his mentor, and he had no doubts about the wisdom of
refusing any university affiliation.

    In the spring and summer of 1969, Fredy spent four months in
Europe. Until mid-May he gave two series of lectures at the Institut
universitaire d'études Européennes in Turin, Italy. One set of lectures was on theories of economic development and the other was
an analysis of economic and social origins of the ghetto.

    At the close of these sessions, Fredy and I traveled to Yugo-
slavia in a small Italian Fiat we bought. A Belgrade friend gave Fredy
his collection of the newspapers *Student* and *Susret* which reported
on the 1968 protests and student uprising in that city. Fredy met with
a number of dissident faculty members from Belgrade University and
also spent some time with friends and former fellow students.

    From Belgrade we went to the Adriatic coast where Fredy used
the verbal and written information acquired in Belgrade to write *Birth
of a Revolutionary Movement in Yugoslavia.**

---

*For the second B & R printing of this pamphlet, in 1973, Fredy changed the title
to *Revolt in Socialist Yugoslavia*.

The small Fiat took us to a number of other European cities in the summer of 1969: Paris, Frankfurt, Florence, London, Amsterdam, Oslo, Copenhagen. In all of them we visited new or old friends, most of them militants—past or potential comrades. Expectation and enthusiasm generated by the 1968 popular uprisings were still high; although the exchange of information and perspectives often focused on disagreements, these meetings were animated by an intensity and camaraderie that by the mid-1970s had diminished to little more than nostalgia.

Eight

Detroit

On our return to the U.S. in August 1969, we settled in Detroit. The choice of Detroit was made largely by eliminating other cities: New York and San Francisco were too expensive, too dominated by rich elites. The midwest industrial centers offered racial and ethnic variety in addition to union-influenced governments. We chose Detroit over Chicago for a relatively small matter: in the fall of 1969 I enrolled as a commuting student at the University of Michigan in Ann Arbor. An advantage of Detroit was that rents in the inner city were cheap. The 1967 riots had caused large numbers of city residents to move to the suburbs.

Without delay we found a comfortable apartment on Gladstone. Its location was not far from where the riots began and even closer to the Algiers Motel, site of the brutal police murders of three black youths in 1967. (By 1969 the motel's name had been changed.) One morning as we were settling into our apartment we heard an ominously loud motorized noise. Going out on the balcony, we saw a tank lumbering up Second Avenue. Two years after the riots the authorities presumably thought the machine could be safely retired.

Fredy was 35 years old when he came to Detroit. He never regretted the move. In many ways this city resembled Belgrade: it was sprawling and unpretentious, a melting-pot for arrivals from other regions, a place where factory work was held in high regard. The image of Detroit as a city of crime-filled streets was not corroborated by our experience, although our car *was* stolen twice.

Within weeks of his arrival in the Motor City, Fredy had made contact with a variety of militants and political groups. In these circles, no one used "We" when referring to U.S. fighting forces in Vietnam. The government's militarism and society's racism were opposed by all these groups, even though they disagreed on what constituted an appropriate course of action. Few of Detroit's activists had heard of *Black & Red,* but they welcomed Fredy, not at all surprised that an unattached intellectual would come to live in Detroit. He found it refreshing to meet people who did not justify their lives in terms of how they made a living.

Facing Reality was a modest publication put out by a group with the same name. In 1969 Marty Glaberman served as a full-time staff person-militant for this left libertarian tendency which had originated as an offshoot of the New York based Workers Party. In the late 1960s and early 1970s, Marty and his wife Jessie furnished unflagging sustenance to people attracted by the non-academic worker-oriented perspectives of Facing Reality. Affiliation with the organization was not a prerequisite for receiving Marty's and Jessie's hospitality. Families with children, not to speak of innumerable American and international visitors, often moved for extended stays into the Glaberman home on Bewick. Detroiters who had their own living quarters would come to do their laundry in the basement machines. The Glaberman dining room accommodated at least twelve persons and the places were often filled. Conversations at the Glabermans' covered many subjects, not all of them directly political. Marty's and Jessie's descriptions of their experiences working in the auto plants fascinated their guests. When Marty told how the workers arranged their on-the-job activity to responsibly fulfill their obligations but still give themselves time for personal projects—known as "government work"—his listeners were always impressed. He gave examples of sensible auto workers taking charge of production on the shop floor in order to correct botched directives by inept managers. Marty always stressed the co-operative nature of factory work. We listeners felt we were getting an inside glimpse of how industrial life really functioned.

With new-found friends from the Facing Reality group, Fredy began his militant activity in Detroit. They wrote a leaflet which began "Who are you? Who Cares?" and which included a brief description of the writers of the leaflet. It was addressed to workers in Detroit and proposed the inauguration of "a publication in which people speak for themselves." The appeal asked workers to contact the leaflet's authors so as to set up communication to initiate the joint project.

Three phone numbers were given.

Fredy's initial optimism, based on the polite—even friendly—response when they passed out the leaflets, turned to disappointment when only one individual actually responded by telephoning. And that person was already "politicized," a member of another organization.

The political theories of another group, News and Letters, were very similar to those of Facing Reality. The intellectual leaders of both groups were originally in the Trotskyist faction of the Workers Party. Raya Dunayevskaya, a former secretary of Trotsky in Mexico and an author who emphasized the Hegelian side of Marxism, was the mentor of News and Letters. She and her followers welcomed Fredy and saw him as a valuable recruit. Some months after meeting him, Raya asked Fredy if he would be willing to edit the book she was writing. Fredy was flattered, but he refused. The cult of personality was practiced too visibly by the News and Letters militants and, after the initial friendly contacts, Fredy had limited contacts with the group.

In 1969 the "underground" newspaper *The Fifth Estate* addressed itself to the Detroit radical and counter-culture community. Fredy sought out the staff and except for a brief period (when there was an attempt to make the paper a commercial success), he was an ardent but critical supporter of the paper, extending his friendship to the numerous remarkable collaborators. In addition to his criticisms, Fredy's typing skills were welcomed. Over the years Fredy took part in the paper's production. At his death in 1985, only one staff person, Marilyn Werbe, had more typesetting seniority than Fredy.

When we arrived in Detroit, the *Fifth Estate* office was on the corner of Warren and the Lodge Freeway. On the floor above lived the White Panther collective who advocated aggressive militancy. One of the ways they practiced it was by procuring guns; the group was pleased to be photographed brandishing them from the rooftop of their headquarters.

Detroit police cars proclaimed their occupants to be "Protectors of Liberty"; "Perpetrators of Violence" would have been a more accurate characterization. The liberty they practiced was their freedom to harass young people who flouted conventions. In the confrontational days of the early 1970s, even the *Fifth Estate's* equipment included a shotgun. Staff members willingly displayed the weapon, but their martial arts were restricted to karate and verbal attacks on government, corporations and their flunkies.

Peter Werbe, *Fifth Estate* stalwart, took Fredy to the adjacent print shop operated by a seventeen-year-old mechanical whiz, Joel Landy. Fredy was impressed by the tall, skinny teenager and often recalled his first view of Joel crawling out from under the gears and rollers of the press he was adjusting. Joel welcomed Fredy, gave him a key, a ten-minute lesson on darkroom techniques and encouraged him to start printing.

Fredy responded eagerly. *Black & Red Number 6½* appeared in the fall of 1969. It was printed in two colors with an innovative layout; it was the last B & R publication for which the text was typewritten. Fredy's contribution, called "The Revolutionary Project," was an illustrated synopsis of *The Reproduction of Daily Life.*

Having access to the *Fifth Estate*'s typesetter, Fredy then prepared and printed his thirty-page essay, *Birth of a Revolutionary Movement in Yugoslavia.* The pamphlet is visually striking. Cartoons and maps appear in several colors. Split fountain, the inking technique which prints a rainbow of colors across the sheet, was in vogue during this period, especially among Joel's friends, and Fredy used it too. The back cover of the 1969 edition carries a logo of a black and a red flag encircled by the words "Revolutionary Printing Co-operative, Detroit."

Collaboration with *Radical America* began at this time. The publication, initially an SDS organ, came out of Madison, Wisconsin. Its editor, Paul Buhle, and its staff were eager to have a "movement" printer produce it. Volume IV, No. 2, their special issue on women, was printed in Joel's print shop in early 1970. The subsequent issue, dated April 1970, was the first publication to emerge from the newly-established Michigan Avenue print shop.

Our early years in Detroit were characterized by frugal living. For a few months we lived on the refund from Fredy's Western Michigan University retirement fund. I had a part-time job teaching math; this paid $100 per month. We got food stamps. Our 1964-model car was a gift from parents. This was the period during which Fredy's father was certain "the Party" was supporting us. "Can't they provide you with health insurance?" he asked.

Our expenses weren't great, little more than $200 per month. As Fredy was preparing to look for a part-time job, a friend working for the state's social service agency made a tempting suggestion. She thought Fredy, with his damaged heart valve, would be eligible for disability welfare payments. She was correct, and for ten years (until the Reagan era) Fredy received modest monthly payments as well as health insurance.

Fredy had no qualms about accepting money from the State. When Peter Werbe smilingly reproached him by saying, "You've got to admit: Life's good in America," Fredy didn't flinch. In fact he viewed his choice to live as a marginal non-consumer to be exemplary; he used his situation to judge others who were willing to sacrifice their personal projects to their wage-earning jobs.

We had frequent guests in our Gladstone apartment. In summer months Fredy treated them to the Czech-style apricot dumplings, knedlecki, for which he won acclaim. In other seasons he made Mexican food. We ate a lot of beans and rice. Meal preparation was always a joint effort and even when visitors were present, Fredy could successfully carry on discussions while he chopped vegetables and stirred sauces. Fredy drank a lot of milk and coffee and he smoked at least two packs of cigarettes every day. He consumed little alcohol and almost never smoked dope, but he did not object when friends smoked dope or drank in our home. He had a very low tolerance for alcohol, probably due to a stomach disorder. He himself found adequate stimulation without alcohol and, although never expressing disapproval of the activity, he spent little time with friends during evenings of heavy drinking.

Fredy's paragraphs on "The Revolutionary Project" in *Black & Red Number 6½* included these sentences: "Men who are chained by their combined daily activities can only be liberated by their combined daily activities. The problem is that the activities that chain men are historically given: their reproduction requires mere repetition; whereas the combined activities that would free men have to be projected: their realization requires creative acts."

Drawn perhaps by *Black & Red*'s earlier publications or perhaps by this challenge, a number of individuals receptive to the Situationist perspective made contact with us. In late 1969 Hannah Ziegellaub and Jon Supak moved to Detroit from New England where they had taken part in actions against Harvard University and in critiques of authoritarian leftists. At the beginning of the new decade Judy and Don Campbell came from Minneapolis. Their arrival brought together the nucleus of a group that established the large printing facility on Michigan Avenue. The impetus for its founding came from a phone call from Bernard Marszalek, a Chicago printer-militant who told Fredy that a complete, but defunct, print shop was being sold.

Along with Carl Smith, a printer and graphic artist who worked with the League of Revolutionary Black Workers, Don, Jon and Fredy went to Chicago, inspected the equipment and arranged for its delivery. While the men were in Chicago, Judy and Hannah sought an industrial loft in which to house the machinery. Numerous people encouraged and aided the project: individuals willing to loan money for the purchase of the equipment were soon found. The needed $4000 for the initial outlay was raised in a few days.

Space for the new printing co-op had to be found quickly. The decision to locate in southwest Detroit across the street from the Cadillac plant and not far from the bridge to Canada came through a connection with the Radical Education Project (REP) which was already established on the second floor of a building in this area. The ground floor was vacant. (The REP collective had moved from Ann Arbor to Detroit in the summer of 1969.)

The prospect of having larger printing equipment as well as darkroom facilities appealed to REP's eight staff people. But they also had some misgivings about having another radical group as a neighbor. Following the split in SDS, REP had become the printing arm of the RYM II* faction and, in 1970, security was one of the collective's primary concerns. (Their paranoia was not groundless. The *Detroit News* had published lurid accounts of their activities and goals, along with their address; threatening phone calls were not uncommon; the police openly kept them under surveillance.) Some of the REP staff were concerned that an amorphous, undisciplined group would be lax about protecting the premises from antagonistic visitors. The first day of our occupancy of the quarters beneath them, REP member Dave Riddle installed chicken wire inside our ground-level windows (as protection against bombs hurled by violent adversaries).

In the ensuing months, energies of dozens of people were directed to the creation of a functioning print shop. Some individuals spent a hundred hours a week there. One of Carl's comrades who worked in a large Detroit printing establishment introduced the company's professional electrician to the enthusiastic co-opers and this man wired the large machines. Other individuals, hearing about the project, found its location and came around to offer services and supplies.

Fredy saw the establishment of the printing co-op as a good example of a "creative act," the sort he had called for in *Black & Red Number 6½,* one he was proud to offer as part of "the com-

*Revolutionary Youth Movement II

bined activities that would free men." The friends and collaborators
who devoted their days and nights to building, operating and maintaining the print shop were altogether confident in their abilities and
did not doubt their success. Although it was necessary to borrow a
substantial sum to buy the equipment, it was recognized that money
was not crucial to the project. Everyone rejected the slightest sug-
gestion that a loan entailed any moral obligation to the donor. In no
case that I can remember did any creditor make claims that his/her
money was responsible for building the print shop.

Practicing his customary methodical approach, Fredy read books
about darkroom design and drew up plans for adjacent darkrooms,
one for each camera. Then the layout of the rest of the shop was
decided on. With the same meticulous care he had used on statistical
analyses in Yugoslav classrooms, Fredy now used flow charts to determine where to place the equipment, the goal being to avoid moving
the paper unnecessarily from the time it was loaded onto the press
until it was packed in boxes at the cutter. (Paper-moving was no trivial
concern. The press printed sheets 22 by 29 inches; in our usual format one sheet contained 24 pages.)

The question of getting wages for working at the printing co-op
was brought up a number of times, especially in the early months
of the shop's existence. REP's staff people received subsistence income. The fact that Fredy received a small monthly payment from
the State made the issue less urgent for him, but even without his
monthly check, it is unlikely that Fredy would have advocated a plan
for wages to be paid. The equipment was old and the people needing
the minimal financial support were far from being skilled printers.
These were considerations, but Fredy's main objection to any arrangement for wages in the co-op was that it would give priority to projects done for money. Fredy wanted the shop to provide the physical
means for innovative ventures and he was convinced that the necessity
to generate wages would conflict with creative (though impractical)
projects. Three or four people made a brief attempt to do "commercial" work from which they would retain a part of the payment, but
they soon gave it up. One co-oper observed that "The capitalists can
transform my labor into money much more efficiently than I can."

Another argument against wages was that the non-paid users of
the shop might see the paid staff as a proletariat responsible for
maintenance and janitorial services. ("After all, you're being paid,
aren't you?") Even with no official staff, some users expected the
mess they left behind to be spirited away by the time they returned

1. The Perlman family in October 1938, shortly before leaving Czechoslovakia. This is possibly their passport photo.

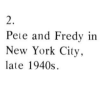

2.
Pete and Fredy in New York City, late 1940s.

3. Fredy on scooter in Yellowstone Park, 1959.

4.
Fredy,
December 1962.

5. Fredy, Velimir Moraca and another student from Economics
Faculty at Belgrade cafe, 1964 or 1965.

6. Lorraine and Fredy on camping trip in Minnesota, Summer 1967.

7.
The nucleus of the
Kalamazoo
Black & Red Gang:
Linda Lanphear,
Fredy, Ursula K.,
Bob Maier,
1969.

8.
Federico Arcos
and Fredy,
1974.

9.
Judy Campbell,
1974.

10. Jeff Gilbert and Fredy at Printing Co-op, 1974.

11. A Social Gathering, March 1979.
Peter Werbe, Carl Saffioti, Alan Franklin, Ralph Franklin, Marilynn Rashid, David Watson, Lorraine, Marilyn Werbe, Tom Mieczkowski, Sue Fraser, Fredy, Dona Saffioti, Pat O'Bryan, Connie Cronin.

12. Fredy in Printing Co-op, 1979.

13. Andy Tymowski, Ann Williams, Lorraine, Fredy, New Haven, 1981.

14. Lorraine, Fredy, Jonathan Fhima, Michele Bloch, Les Halles, Paris, 1984.

15.
Fredy and
Marilynn Rashid
in an Ontario
campground,
July 1985.

16. Lorraine and Fredy, June 1985.

on the following day. Misconceptions of this sort were quickly cleared up.

By the summer of 1970 guidelines for using the printing co-op had been discussed and agreed upon. A price list was prepared so users would know the cost of supplies and overhead. The price list also made explicit some of the principles of the shop's builders:

—The equipment of the Printing Co-op is social property. It is and shall be controlled by all individuals who need, use and maintain it.

—It is not and shall not be owned or controlled by any individual or group of individuals, whether they claim to serve, represent, or speak for society, whether they are elected or self-appointed.

—The purpose of the Printing Co-op is to provide access to printing equipment to all those individuals in the community who desire to express themselves (on a non-profit basis), with charges made only to maintain the print shop (rent, utilities, materials, maintenance of the machinery).

—It is not the purpose of the Printing Co-op to solve the problem of unemployment, nor to provide business opportunities for enterprising capitalists.

Fredy was exhilarated by all aspects of the new activity. During the initial years of the Printing Co-op he frequently asserted that never before had he felt so *intellectually* stimulated as he was by the challenges and gratifications he found in mastering the graphic arts equipment and techniques. In this period he appreciated machines, and would have liked a Heidelberg press in the Printing Co-op. He realized that some of the flaws in his ambitious color experiments were due to shortcomings of the Harris press and he frequently reminded others that we were using fifty-year-old technology and equipment.

Fredy's appreciation of machines caused him to admire individuals who understood them. Mechanical skills are so visible, so hard to simulate, that it was easy to separate the "big talkers" from the "doers." The talents of Paul W., one of the "doers," were called upon from the first to the final days of the co-op. It was a pleasure to watch Paul's systematic approach to a malfunctioning machine. Without comment, haste or intervention, he would observe the belts and gears from all angles; like a chess player, he studied how an adjustment at one point would affect another function. On one occasion he found the explanation for a paper feeding problem on the press to be a loose connection in the electrical box.

Paul did not disparage his skills, but did not consider them overly remarkable. He took more pride in another contribution he made to the print shop. Following a bid of about $500 at an auction of a bankrupt print shop, he acquired for the co-op an enormous supply of film, plates and darkroom supplies. One "lot" of panchromatic film permitted Fredy, sometimes with Carl Smith, sometimes with me, to experiment with color reproduction without thought to expense of supplies. Some of the film remained usable and unopened until 1980.

Paul liked the camaraderie of his political associates, but the implications of their slogans and ideology failed to excite him. Initially on the REP staff, he left that collective to organize an auto co-op, but after a couple of years gave that up. He stayed around political circles until a commitment he made to bind (by hand) thousands of books turned into an exploitative situation; he became bitter about his labor being taken lightly and very suspicious of smooth-talking militants. When he moved away from the neighborhood, he had the intention of becoming a professional gambler.

In the early 1970s there was a modest resurgence of the IWW (Industrial Workers of the World). Once the Printing Co-op was established, Fredy and many other participants became members of the IWW; for several years we pasted the dues stamps into our little red membership books. A union "bug" which incorporated the IWW emblem was designed by Fredy for the Printing Co-op. It read "Abolish the State. Abolish Wage Labor."

The revival of interest in the Wobblies, whose traditions and history were respected by most U.S. leftists, was partially due to the fragmentation of SDS and the anti-war movement. A number of the most active SDS militants, too impatient to join a struggle which might go on for decades, had studied successful revolutionary movements in China, Cuba and Russia and took the leaders of these movements as their models. The decrees of Kim Il Sung were admired; Mao was quoted and his aphorisms analyzed; solidarity with the Cuban revolution was demonstrated by going to the island to harvest sugar cane. Theoretical grounding for the projects of most militants came, however, from the 1917 revolution in Russia when the Bolsheviks seized power. Party-building under the auspices of a clandestine core of individuals was taken as the authentic model for revolutionary

activity. Rival groups of militants carefully chose slogans to communicate their perspective. Bellicose Weathermen fought with bathers
at Metropolitan Beach in suburban Detroit. The less violent RYM
II faction's sinister side could be seen in its adherence to Leninist
and Stalinist principles; paranoia and policing were central to its
pronouncements.

A few ambitious militants saw the newly established print shop
as a facility which could further what they considered an urgent and
politically correct social program. Fredy was highly sensitive to
manipulators and potential bureaucrats, so individuals who approached
the Printing Co-op "proletariat" offering leadership quickly learned
Fredy's opinion about their "correct line." Few of them could with-
stand for long Fredy's scathing denunciations, although one thick-
skinned Stalinist was remarkably tenacious. In the end, Pat's chances
were ruined by his assumption that Carl Smith shared the Leninist
prejudices of his comrades at Black Star (the printing and media wing
of the League of Revolutionary Black Workers), and would welcome
a purge of undisciplined libertarians. Pat confidently and confiden-
tially assured Carl that the anarchists would soon be ousted from the
Printing Co-op. But Carl had no complaints about his fellow
co-opers—the people Pat called "anarchists" — and he warned us of
the manipulative intentions. The confrontation came sooner than Pat
expected and its outcome was the opposite of what he had predicted.
The hostile encounter was mercifully brief.

Fredy's insulting intolerance of schemes proposed by self-
proclaimed comrades kept the printing co-op from becoming institu-
tionalized, but another result was a fair bit of eloquent vilification.
Not every newcomer was guilty of manipulative scheming. Alan
Franklin, in a letter written a number of years later, criticized Fredy's
propensity to suspect the worst of some people. Alan reproached Fredy
for

> your consistent attribution of the basest motives imaginable to
> people with whom you have differences. Your capacity to see
> villainy in the most ambiguous of actions, and your willingness
> to believe the worst of those with whom you've had run-ins,
> attain at times the level of what I can only describe as genuine
> paranoia.
> . . .
> [Y]our responses. . . reflect, to me, a consistent pattern of mental
> aggrandizement of the offending party in which, the greater your
> anxiety at the situation, the larger the evil figure looms in your

mind—and the more intense a campaign of slander and vilification you mount to neutralize the threat...

Fredy and his "paranoia" may have chased away some individuals,
but the print shop did not become a "resource" for a political party.
Conformity to ideological principles was not required in order to use
the printing equipment. People who disapproved of this openness frequently formulated their objection with the question, "But what if
fascists come and ask to use the equipment?" This dilemma was never
encountered. Certain ideological purists nevertheless considered the
printing project, as well as Black & Red's publishing project, tainted
because of our association with people whose political outlook differed from ours. Fredy answered one such accusation in a letter written
in January 1971:

> [Y]ou define as my enemies the "Maoists" and others with whom
> I cooperatively share printing equipment, but whose perspec-
> tives I don't share. You're wrong. There is of course the
> possibility that "Maoists" will one day exclude me from access
> to the printing equipment unless I "appropriate the coherence
> of their critique" and until I "correct" my "errors." But until today
> such a threat has not come from "Maoists." Your argument
> against working with people who have "wrong" perspectives (or
> "bad politics") merely demonstrates that with words it is possible
> to make *anything* sound anti-bureaucratic and ultra-democratic:
> even a perspective according to which "appropriation of the
> critique" of the Situationist International is a precondition for
> access to social means of production. But, you know, only a
> large Thought Police and a highly organized bureaucratic terror
> can assure such unanimity among the producers.

In the last years of its existence, when few groups other than
Black & Red took advantage of the co-op's facilities, Fredy was less
sanguine about the far-reaching success of the printing project, but
in the early 1970s, Fredy was elated by its achievements. The
darkroom facilities were immediately used to make REP's negatives.
Fredy, with help from others, printed the essay on C. Wright Mills,
The Incoherence of the Intellectual; we reprinted the *Reproduction
of Daily Life* pamphlet and his 1962 play, *Plunder.* Jon Supak and
Marilyn Keydel published a 70-page excerpt from Raoul Vaneigem's
*The Revolution of Daily Life.** Black Star printed *The Political*

Traité de savoir-vivre à l'usage des jeunes générations.

Thought of James Foreman. Peter Allen, an anarchist printer from Chicago came to print his *Prolegomena.*

The participation of two groups particularly pleased Fredy. One was from Cass High School, students antagonized by the coercive aspects of that institution. With minimal help from people older than themselves, Hughthir White, Stuart Shevin, Raymond Davis, John Hock and their friends succeeded in printing their unofficial newspaper, *Red Star.* The equipment was just as recalcitrant for people under sixteen as for those over sixteen, but at least two issues of their paper came out of the Michigan Avenue print shop.

The second group had literary and artistic interests. The printing efforts of these gifted, articulate intellectuals were concentrated on producing a high-quality magazine, *riverrun* (the word with which James Joyce commenced *Finnegans Wake*). They were themselves the authors of the stories, poems and essays featured in their journal; photographs of original paintings and drawings also appeared. They took great care with layout and design and were willing to spend whatever time was needed in order to emerge from the darkroom with a well-made halftone. The irreverent put-downs and the witty banter of Alan Franklin, Gus Hellthaler, John Grant, Marty Fischhoff, Sam Levy and Ralph Franklin enlivened the shop's atmosphere. It was a welcome change from the political rhetoric or the technical language that usually prevailed. Fredy admired their wit as well as the handsome journals they produced. Over a two-year period, there were three issues of *riverrun.*

Fredy did not count among the print shop's remarkable successes the printing achievements of Hamish Sinclair and his political comrades, but he considered their cordial cooperation to be exemplary. Fredy and I had known Hamish as one of the Living Theatre activists in New York City in the early 1960s. The prior acquaintance and Hamish's sense of humor made it easy to welcome him and his group to the print shop. Hamish was serious about learning to print; he respected the machines and became a competent printer. He and his comrades were responsible users of the shop; they fulfilled their financial obligations and put in many hours working on *Radical America.* Their own project at the co-op was to print a newspaper directed to factory workers. Eventually they discovered that commercial printers could furnish them with copies (on newsprint) faster and cheaper than they could print them themselves. But they still used the light tables and darkroom facilities and continued to share maintenance responsibility.

The political orientation of the group was pro-Stalinist and the texts they printed extolled the virtues of the Soviet Union. In spite of their differences, Fredy's and Hamish's political discussions were generally quite friendly; neither attempted to convert the other. We occasionally ate meals together at which time we exchanged views on events and personalities. Hamish's comrades seemed to avoid verbal confrontations with Fredy and, on philosophic issues, to shun exchanges of any kind. Fredy wondered if they had been instructed to merely nod and keep quiet.

Once there was an exception. At the end of a meal prepared by Barbara Martin and Hamish, Fredy was applying his anti-authoritarian perspective in order to criticize the institutions and behavior of contemporary leftist groups. Barbara objected that Fredy did not give enough credit to the dissidents' good intentions and was too critical of their methods for recruiting workers. She insisted that it was legitimate to appeal to workers' nationalistic sentiments. As the conversation became heated, Fredy brought out the example of the German National Socialists whose hateful practices falsified their initial, admirable-sounding goals. Barbara was not able to argue against Fredy's example. She may not even have been aware that the political party Fredy was denouncing was commonly known as "the Nazis," but she was not willing to accept Fredy's objections. Her retort stopped Fredy cold. It was the only time I can remember Fredy at a loss for words. Her accusation brought the discussion to a very personal level: "Oh, you Germans just have a *thing* about authority."

Fredy had his revenge. An illustration in the first edition of Michael Velli's *Manual for Revolutionary Leaders* showed the rejected debris of the repressive old regime; included in the garbage was Barbara's and Hamish's paper, *r.p.m.* Barbara was probably impervious to this insult, but Hamish was hurt. This antagonistic gesture was not in keeping with the conventions of our collaboration at the print shop.

In the period when the Michigan Avenue shop was put together, commercial printing establishments commonly practiced censorship; this meant that there was no assurance that a text or a poster could be published. Many people recognized the truth of the statement, "Freedom of the press is guaranteed only to those who own one," and gave encouragement and support to the collective project. Some brought donations of furniture or supplies; others offered concrete skills; some just came around to watch others work on a purposeful, non-commercial activity; very few sought control. But there were some among these print shop supporters whose attitude antagonized people building and working in the shop. They approached us like consultants, often had a condescending attitude and sometimes suggested that their contributions could be repaid at some future date in either tangible or intangible ways. They seemed to hope that their moral support, the public relations value of their verbal encouragement, or their furnishing us with texts to print qualified them to be considered fellow workers in the project. Although most moral supporters and consultants were given keys and not treated rudely, indifference was the usual response to their offers.

The best documented clarification of such misconceptions about the co-op occurred in 1973, three years after the shop had been established (and after sensitivity had been increased as a result of earlier encounters). When Black & Red was preparing to reprint Rubin's *Essays on Marx's Theory of Value,* we accepted the proposal of Dimitri Roussopoulos, editor of the Montreal-based Black Rose Books, to print five hundred additional copies with the Black Rose logo on the cover and the title page. Dimitri's attitude was, in fact, clear in his initial letter of March 1, 1973 but we overlooked the assertion that *he* was doing *us* the favor: "Black Rose Books would also like to help by buying...300 copies [of the Rubin book]...at cost of production to you."

The arrangement proved quite satisfactory to Dimitri and later that year when the translation of Arshinov's *History of the Makhnovist Movement* was ready to be printed, Dimitri proposed that Black Rose appear as co-publisher of this book as well. We agreed to print one thousand copies with their logo. Shortly before the actual printing got underway, Dimitri sent a hastily-written letter with a number of requests and instructions; some of these were trivial, but others, like changing the book's title, were totally unacceptable. Fredy wrote an angry reply, indignant about Dimitri's senseless instructions to send unbound books "not in signatures," ridiculing the changed title (to "Black Ukraine") and objecting to a proposed statement for the back cover. He also returned the $500 check which had been sent as partial payment.

Dimitri wrote a defensive reply claiming that his earlier letter had been written in haste because he was "in the middle of a number of other things." After defending his earlier proposals, Dimitri concluded, "I think that it is strictly out of order to throw piety and self-righteousness at each other, as to who is poorer, who is more anti-capitalist and non-commercial. . . It is up to you if you feel you want to cut off all our relationship *[sic]* and common projects. We urge you to reconsider."

Fredy reconsidered the earlier relationship, regretted it and, angered by Dimitri's defensive apology, wrote him a four-page letter in which he tried to disabuse Dimitri of the assumption that the earlier "collaboration" (on Rubin's book) could be characterized as a "common project":

> You refer to your purchase of 500 (or 600) copies of Rubin's book as a precedent, a sort of model, of "our relationship," and you refer to this transaction as a "common project," and thus as a basis for our present and future relations.
>
> I think you should know that we did not regard our relation with you over the Rubin books as a "common project," but rather as something quite opposite from that. Your letter of November 8 made it clear to us that you were not only completely insensitive to the absolute one-sidedness of this relationship, but that, on the contrary, you were ready to make the very worst elements of that relationship a basis for present and future "collaboration" with us.

The entire letter is reproduced in the Appendix; it provides a good example of Fredy's argumentative skills while documenting some of the tasks and concerns associated with the print shop. One aspect of the letter needs a comment, I think. Fredy's description of the co-op's financial straits is misleading; it was never in "desperate" need of money, although the binding machine was purchased with money borrowed from friends. This comment should not, however, be interpreted as minimizing the indignation we felt when, after furnishing supplies and doing much manual work, we were not paid for the finished publications until months later.

Ambiguities about a "common project" were absent from our relations with the *Radical America* staff. They furnished camera-ready copy, pre-addressed envelopes, and mailing lists. They were conscientious about fulfilling their obligations and, with one exception, we were too. (Since there was a page available in one of the first issues of *Radical America* printed in Detroit—an issue devoted to papers read at the fifth Socialist Scholars' Conference—Paul Buhle suggested that we use it to print an announcement about Black & Red. It did not occur to Paul to ask to see it before it was included.

Our graphic and text were a put-down of Marxist scholars who sought
merely to *interpret* the world, and suggested that B & R's goal was
to *change* the world.)

In addition to covering costs of the publication, money from
Radical America paid a good part of the shop's rent and utilities —
about half of what was needed. Printing an issue of *Radical America*
was a labor-intensive activity; it usually took about two weeks. Fredy
and I were responsible for the darkroom work, printing and folding.
Many others came to help with the collating, binding and mailing.
Some of the first issues printed in Detroit had multiple flaws; for-
tunately, our printing skills improved over the years. We maintained
cordial relations with Jim O'Brien, who replaced Paul Buhle as coor-
dinator. Jim occasionally came through Detroit and once spent two
weeks here helping to print, bind and mail one issue of the journal.

In 1969 Roger Gregoire and Linda Lanphear had gone to Paris
intending to continue collaborating on Black & Red projects from
there, but they were soon concentrating their attention on the Situationist International (SI), exposing the ideological differences between
French leftists and the SI, an organization they were eager to join.
Some of Black & Red's earlier activity in Kalamazoo did not conform to the exacting Situationist principles, and certain ideological
guardians of the SI viewed askance the openness of the current printing
project in Detroit. According to the ideologues, the most essential
political task was to clarify differences between Situationist theory
and the perspectives of other leftists. Past association with non-
Situationist activists would have to be repudiated before Linda and
Roger could be considered worthy of admission to the SI's inner circle.
If past errors were acknowledged and if the confessions conformed
to the SI's requirements, the gatekeepers held out hope that Roger
and Linda could become participants in the "international revolutionary
movement," namely, become members of the SI.

Roger's and Linda's repudiation of past errors took the form of
long letters addressed to Fredy but submitted to SI officials as proof
of their current convictions. In the letters they reproached Fredy for
associating with people in Kalamazoo who lacked even the slightest
knowledge of the Situationist critique; the letters pointed out that by
printing *Radical America* in Detroit he was continuing his incorrect
practice. They urged him to recognize the flaws of Kalamazoo
associates, to break off relations with *Radical America* as well as
with all Detroiters who had conventional leftist views and to make

the break public by composing, printing and distributing an open letter in which his repudiation would be unambiguously stated.

Fredy was deeply hurt by the letters and disappointed in his friends. He was hurt because the Kalamazoo collaboration had been so congenial; Fredy considered the printing projects and the university interventions to have been exemplary acts. The letters distorted what Fredy considered the reality of their shared activity. He was disappointed in his friends' willingness to humiliate themselves; it was *their* past they were denouncing as well as his. He had expected them to carry out autonomous projects in Paris, similar to ones they had creatively defined in Kalamazoo. Their letters made him question if the past activity of these individuals had really been so admirable if they could now be accepting purges and advocating ideological purity.

Outrage was another of Fredy's responses to the letters and the one that permeated his reply which began:

Dear Aparatchiki,
     Your recent letters would have meant much more if a carbon of one and the original of the other had not been sent to a functionary of the Situationist International as part of an application for membership. The logic of your arguments would be impressive if it had not been designed to demonstrate your orthodoxy in Situationist doctrine. The sincerity of your "rupture with Fredy Perlman and Black and Red" would be refreshing if it had not been calculated to please a Priest of a Church which demands dehumanizing confessions as a condition for adherence. You're a toady.
     The odor is made more unpleasant by the fact that you chose to approach the Situationist International precisely in its period of great purges (Khayati, Chasse, Elwell, Vaneigem, Etc.). Some people joined the Communist Party precisely at the time of Stalin's great purges.

In a later paragraph Fredy turns one of their complaints against him into an attack of the S.I.:

[I]n your letters you refer to my avoidance of the problem of Organization. You're wrong. I avoid being sucked into organizations of professional specialists in "revolution"; apparently you desire to be sucked in. We disagreed about this in Kalamazoo as well, but with this difference: you did not at that time demand unanimity as a basis for working together. To avoid being sucked into such organizations is not the same as to avoid the problem of being sucked in. Unfortunately, seen through the 3-D glasses you're wearing today I'm again missing the point. I'm talking about *all other bureaucratic* organizations, not about the Situationist International. Its bureaucrats aren't bureaucrats. Its purges aren't purges. Its ideology is not ideology: it is practice; whose practice? the anti-bureaucratic practice of the proletarians; this is the practice that justifies the intimidations, insults, confessions, purges which are necessary to keep the Coherence coherent. This Organization is unique: unlike all the Stalinist Parties, unlike the Second, Third and Fourth Internationals, the Situationist International is itself the world revolutionary movement, so that one does not apply to Verlaan for membership but for "an autonomous positive existence within the international revolutionary movement" (your letter to Verlaan).

The break with Linda and Roger made Fredy even more skeptical that a shared ideological perspective was in itself an adequate basis for undertaking common projects, and it made him decidedly unreceptive to alignments with adherents of Situationism. One young Californian, who had been rejected by the west coast American wing of the SI and who was looking elsewhere for comrades with Situationist views, found our apartment on Gladstone and knocked on the door, expecting to be welcomed. Extending his hand while introducing himself, he confidently assured Fredy, "We have everything in common!" Had the newcomer said, "I've come to Detroit to learn how to print!" it's likely he would have been welcomed. But Fredy had heard reports about the California milieu from which the man emerged, wanted no part in the ideological squabbles rending it and squelched the visitor's expectations by responding, "Name *one* thing!"

Ironically, at the time this young man was seeking Situationist comrades in Detroit, the group he wanted to "join" had just undertaken a collective project to translate into English the text which was the cornerstone of Situationist theories: Guy Debord's *La Société du Spectacle.* The translating sessions, attended by Hannah, Jon, Judy, Don, Fredy and me, usually turned into commentary on the author's observations. We all found examples to illustrate the truth of his theories, frequently citing our experiences in establishing a print shop without recourse to hierarchy or bureaucracy. As a model of collaborative activity, this translating effort had visible flaws. When there were differences on how to formulate a passage, it was usually Fredy's version that was finally accepted. Fredy's stubbornness occasionally seemed unkind but when he firmly believed that his choice was better, he refused to give way. He felt that accepting an inferior formulation in order to protect another's self-image was doing a disservice to the common project as well as behaving condescendingly to the individual. The disagreements, in fact, were rarely substantive. A typical one centered on the word "cleavage." Jon objected to using the word in the context of Debord's analysis because to him "cleavage" suggested only a feature of a woman's body.

Debord's book was profoundly understood by all of us who worked first on translating it and then printing it. Although the Situationists' "coherence of the critique" was viewed skeptically (as a potential rigid ideology) and a photo of the French Situationists was included in the chapter that denounces self-appointed centralized decision-making, translating Debord's book was a rewarding activity for us in the Detroit of 1970.

Of the six of us, none was more determined or more successful in finding creative responses to life in Detroit than Judy Campbell. Extremely sensitive to and resentful of arbitrary authority, she was confident that others in the integrated, vibrant and rebellious Motor City would quickly see through the absurdities that camouflage unjust social relations. She also had great confidence in her ability to define and carry out projects.

Judy installed plumbing in the print shop darkroom, she helped typeset the Debord translation and provided excellent halftone negatives of the graphics she chose to accompany the text; she was a good cook, a responsible housemate, a responsive listener. She read very little and never quoted authors to support an argument, but ideas stimulated her and she incorporated new theories into her "rap." For a year or more she had been a student at MIT in Cambridge, Massachusetts, but she rejected the university and scorned people who took academic learning seriously.

Judy and her husband Don separated about a year after they came to Detroit and Don moved away. Once the print shop was complete and functioning, Judy spent little time there. She was fascinated by Detroit and wanted to be a participant in its elusive vitality. In 1971 she got a job with the post office and, as mail carrier, had ample opportunity to observe inner-city neighborhoods. After the mail was delivered she spent long hours in bars with other postal workers. She didn't patronize them; they were her friends. Neither did she model

herself in their image. Spectator sports didn't interest her and she
never became a baseball fan. Far from being a prude, she had many
lovers and consistently refused monogamous relationships. Judy did
not venture into the underworld of crime and drugs. Most of her
friends were workers, most of them black. The few I met seemed
apolitical and eager to enjoy available pleasures; they admired and
respected Judy but seemed to think it unlikely that she would be a
permanent part of their lives.

After a couple years of "hard living," Judy was less interested
in mingling with Detroit's working class. She stopped working for
the post office, recouped her forces and turned to more specific projects. Some theater and film productions, which she and Highland
Park friends had presented, led her to rent and equip (with help from
others) a storefront which could serve as a theater facility. Easy Space,
as it was called, provided the setting for a number of original theatrical
works in the mid-1970s. Unstinting in her efforts, Judy grew increasingly critical of the merely verbal commitments of some of the other
participants. Antagonisms grew, and accusations of manipulation,
unfair appropriation and exploitation became more vehement. One
faction of the theater group found a storefront near Wayne University where they could present their plays, and the Easy Space project came to an end.

Judy's response to a disagreeable incident gives an idea of her
outlook and her practice. One summer night following a downtown
street fair, Judy and her close friend Richard were returning to their
car. A group of exuberant black youths accosted them, ridiculed them,
hurled epithets and finally chased them. The experience distressed
Judy, not so much for its violence (the male and female teenagers
had no weapons), but because she, who had put much effort into being
a Detroiter, hadn't succeeded in talking to them, in making them
recognize a common bond. She resented being lumped with the
suburban outsiders from whom Judy considered herself readily
distinguishable.

This incident made Judy question whether her efforts to be part
of the city had failed. Her principles were at stake. She would not
see herself as a victim, helpless in the face of thoughtless racial
categorization.

She composed a reply to the insults hollered by the young people.
It began: "From the 'White Bitch' " and was addressed to "The Young
People who chased two individuals in downtown Detroit last Satur-
day night." She printed hundreds of copies, then distributed them

in various neighborhoods. Some she posted on light poles, but most she personally handed to residents. The ensuing conversations restored Judy's confidence in the correctness of her principles even though the memory of that unpleasant event was not effaced.

Judy made efforts to *change* the world in which she lived. She and Fredy agreed on fundamental approaches and each had respect for the other, even when they no longer collaborated on projects. They both recognized the importance of changing one's own situation, and both were extremely sensitive to glib talk, detesting individuals who proposed mammoth transformations but who did nothing. In choosing friends and forming judgments, they both had an unusual ability to ignore a person's social prestige (or lack of it), age, sex and background.

Judy, like Fredy, was a severe judge of her own activities, seeing them as exemplary acts. She also made rigorous demands on her friends and, when they didn't live up to her expectations, felt betrayed. Judy's expectations were based on her confident assumption that others shared her insights and her skills. Unlike Fredy, who was fifteen years her senior and who retained a deep-rooted philosophical and literary perspective, these repeated disappointments took a great toll on Judy's spirit. The scope of her projects diminished, the bitterness she harbored toward former friends became increasingly visible and in 1981 she left Detroit.

The early 1970s saw a surge of fervent attempts to undermine consumerism and social conventions and Judy was not unique in trying to live according to her principles. Members of the Boone's Farm commune were more political than those from other hippie groups in the Cass Corridor area of Detroit but just as outrageously unconventional in appearance. Many took part in *Fifth Estate* and printing co-op activities. With them we discussed the political implications of communal living as well as problems common to their Avery Street house and printing cooperatives. Occasionally Fredy and I were invited to a communal dinner. We looked pretty "straight" in the midst of bare feet and tangled hair but never felt discriminated against. To us the Boone's Farm commune seemed a jolly and stimulating place to live.*

The hippie lifestyle was adopted by choice, not necessity. Some political militants found a sober, ascetic style more appropriate to

*In the early 1970s Fredy stopped cutting his hair. To keep it from getting caught in the press rollers, he wore a rubber band around it and continued to keep it in a pony tail long after our Detroit hippie friends cut and groomed their hair.

their temperaments. These martyr-prone militants were often congenial fellow workers, but their self-sacrifice inhibited close friendships. One such comrade lived without a car in one of the city's desolate corners which was barely served by Detroit's bus system, but well-provided with teenage gangs. She lived through a Michigan winter without heat or a phone, too committed to her political work to abandon it for a job that would provide an income.

Unlike many flower children who in this period moved to rural areas in an effort to find a more congenial environment, such martyrs for a higher cause did not reject modern "comforts" on principle, or question industrial production. Their tolerance for discomfort, combined with their expectation that the sacrifices would, at some future date, be recognized as moral achievements and rewarded materially, provided us with insights about the personal dimension in the transformation traced in Michael Velli's *Manual for Revolutionary Leaders*. The lifestyle chosen by these political dissidents also corroborated analyses of Wilhelm Reich and Maurice Brinton.

We printed the latter's *The Irrational in Politics* at the printing co-op. Typesetting and layout were done by *Fifth Estate* friends who shared our view of sacrifice.

Detroit was a popular stop for traveling militants in the early 1970s. The 1967 rebellion was recent history, militant workers — both black and white — were vocal, the Motown image hadn't faded; the mini-parties set up by leftist organizers provided numerous nonestablishment papers and journals.* The printing co-op was on the itinerary of many political tourists from Europe as well as North America.

Some Detroit political groups were eager to attract recruits and they offered hospitality to local and out-of-town visitors. In addition to giving them a tour of the print shop, one cell leader (no advocate of postponing earthly joys) took the potential comrades (male) to call on some of the young women active in Detroit's counter culture. He wanted the recruits to see what the leftist milieu offered in the way of partners. The women, naive at first, quickly found a nonrevolutionary label for this resourceful recruiter and distanced themselves from his exploitative hospitality.

---

*Already then, the sense of destiny harbored by some of these leftists seemed quaint. Even those disinclined to title their paper *The Spark* (Lenin's newspaper), were careful to keep a file of the early issues of their paper. They found it at least plausible that "after the revolution" their paper would be credited with fomenting the decisive North American uprising; they wanted the documents to be preserved.

In the summer of 1971 Fredy and I took a trip to Alaska. My
sister Ruth and a wilderness-loving friend, Debbie Hunsberger,
accompanied us. We went in a sturdy Chevrolet loaded with spare
tire and camping gear. Our average speed on the Alaska Highway
through the Yukon was under 20 miles per hour due partly to the
bumpy road, partly to frequent stops to admire the spectacular scenery.
Two weeks after setting out, we reached Fairbanks.

When we saw the sign on the outskirts, "Fairbanks, All-American
City," we laughed. This was as untypical an American city as we
could imagine. We were appalled by the structures; it looked like
a shoddy frontier town and people seemed poor. Young, unemployed
men were waiting around for construction to get underway on the
gas/oil pipeline.

A brief stay in Fairbanks convinced Fredy that the "all-American
city" label was apt. This Alaskan town in 1971 was a replica of a
myriad of other North American cities from an earlier era. One sensed
that its inhabitants hated the environment around them. Their structures were made from imported materials, asphalt was laid down on
undulating tundra; neon lights and billboards interfered with the view
of the mountains. Fairbanks was a blight which was devouring its
surroundings.

Ten years later, Fredy saw Phoenix, Arizona with the same eyes:
humans stubbornly insisted on lawns and trees in an environment
where clover lawns and woodland trees destroyed nature's balance.
The former blooming desert had been reduced to a familiar, but
odious, urban sprawl. By then, he saw all cities as ugly encroachments
created by arrogant subjugators who were assisted by fully consenting
underlings.

The trip to Alaska marked a change in Fredy's view of the society
he lived in. He began asking whether human intervention was ever
benign. He had a new perception of cities and urban activities, and
looked at Progress with a more critical eye. A few years later, when
he read Jacques Camatte's *Invariance* in which the French follower
of Amadeo Bordiga attributes the loss of human community to
domestication by Capital, Fredy was pleased to discover insights which
clarified his evolving appraisal of Western (and Marxist) assumptions about Progress. It would be five years before Fredy started
preparing himself for a systematic critique of Progress, but his antagonism to giant industrial processes was growing more explicit.

Nine

Exposing the Rackets

The most pressing need in 1972, in Fredy's view, was to discredit manipulative political organizers. Libertarian-sounding programs contained implicit assumptions which Fredy was determined to expose. When someone shouted "All Power to the People!" Fredy heard "All Power to the Leader!" He wanted to justify the accuracy of his perception by documenting past transformations of one slogan into the other; he also wanted to trace the logic which prompted his leftist contemporaries to follow the same trajectory.

Neither transformation was hard to document. Leaders of successful revolutions in this century were prolific writers and, without exception, viewed their taking up the reins of power as a reasonable outcome of a desire to "Serve the People." By 1970, most New Leftists in the United States saw Leninist-type parties (Russian, Cuban, Chinese) as a prerequisite for revolution in this country, and they were applying their predecessors' tactics to the American situation. Few of the young radicals were familiar with dissenters from the revolutionary outcome or even with any of the victorious leaders' fallen rivals, and they unabashedly identified with Fidel, Mao, Ho and Lenin.

Fredy and I compiled quotes from the writings of these New Leftists and the leaders they were trying to emulate. We arranged them in a logical sequence and presented them as a *Manual for Revolutionary Leaders*. Michael Velli was alleged to be the author of this text. The logic of power-seeking turned a statement by Hitler, Mussolini, Ho or Lenin into an appropriate conclusion to a paragraph begun by New Left militants writing in *The Guardian, New Left Notes* or other journals.

The purpose of this compilation was to criticize the direction of our contemporaries' radical activity. We assumed that when the lust for power was shown to result inescapably from the development of the leftists' mild-sounding starting principles, the goal of seeking state power would be discredited. It turned out that we were naive. An alarming number of readers missed the point and in the second printing of M. Velli's *Manual* we listed the sources of the quotes. If readers were going to aspire to state power, we wanted them to identify correctly their successful predecessors. The documentation is introduced as follows:

> M. Velli's thought is a synthesis of the ideas of the major revolutionary leaders of the age... Velli has taken all of these ideas out of the contexts in which they first appeared and placed them into the single Thought of which each of these ideas is a mere fragment. [p.263]

The citations from texts of successful and aspiring revolutionary leaders form Chapter Two of the *Manual for Revolutionary Leaders* and is entitled "The Rise to Leadership." This chapter advises the militant about only one stage on the road to success. Fredy wrote Chapters One and Three to complete the picture. "Generation of Revolutionaries," Chapter One, gives a brief history of capitalist development; it focuses on the growing alienation and disaffection which unnerve present-day state authorities. In Chapter Three, "The Seizure of State Power," Fredy incorporates other quotes into a sobering description of the demise of a revolution. The vignettes at the beginning of the chapter illustrate Fredy's hopeful vision of how authority can be resisted; then he shows how seemingly trivial acts of acquiescence imply renunciation of one's "self-powers." The *Manual* ends with the victory of the Leader/Prince, the reestablishment of law and order (the police apparatus remains intact; the legal structure revises nothing but terminology) and the work concludes with Machiavelli exhorting his superior to Study War.

In composing graphics for the *Manual* we tried to make the same argument as in the text. The beginnings of paragraphs in Book Two feature faces of revolutionary leaders. Stalin, Trotsky and Lenin are the saints displayed on Russian icons; the reign of a leader and commodities signifies the success of revolutionary materialism; the state —

brazenly mobilizing its subjects like sheep—appears as the preeminent object for worship in contemporary society. More than half of the graphics are printed in color; most are formed from collages. The 261-page *Manual* was printed in 1972.

The same year we also printed *Essays on Marx's Theory of Value* by the Soviet economist I.I. Rubin. The author had been imprisoned by Stalin, and his book removed from Soviet libraries. Miloš Samardžija, Fredy's Yugoslav professor and co-translator of the book, considered Rubin's exposition of Marx's theory of commodity fetishism to be excellent and wanted to make it available to contemporary readers.* Black & Red undertook to print the translation after attempts to find a university or commercial publisher had failed. Fredy's essay on commodity fetishism, written in 1967, served as introduction to the English edition.

In the spring of 1973 we moved to a row house on Porter Street, in southwest Detroit. The move was preceded by a rent strike against the greedy slum landlord who had recently bought the four-apartment Gladstone building. Our new home was less than two miles from the print shop which was now accessible by bicycle or even by foot. By Detroit standards, the building we moved into was old and somewhat shabby, but it gave us a lot more space. We had an extra room for guests, a room for chamber music and a small back yard where Fredy planted a vegetable garden. Immediately following our move, Fredy spent some weeks painting and outfitting the house. Using the landlord's power tools, he built sturdy kitchen cabinets, assembled shelving and tables to complete an alcove for the light table, and built cabinets for Black & Red supplies. Absent from the house on Porter Street, as from all our previous residences, was a television.

The ten years we lived on Porter Street were sociable ones. Many friends lived nearby and we exchanged frequent visits. Bob Maier, Hughthir White, Tanya Sharon, Terri and Kemal Orcan, Patti Keyes, Don Kirkland and Paul W. were among our immediate neighbors. Marilyn and Jeff Gilbert and Judy Campbell lived minutes away.

People living in this area of Detroit—largely, but not entirely, of Mexican or Appalachian background—formed a rudimentary community. Our affection for "the community" would reach a low ebb

---

*When Samardžija, on a visit to the Soviet Union, went to the National Library and asked to see Rubin's book (which was listed in the catalog), a security officer escorted him from the building and warned him not to return. Subsequently Fredy found a copy of the Russian original in the U.S. Library of Congress.

when midnight drag races were held on Porter Street or when
neighbors (or passers-by) imposed on us blaring rock music from
their ghetto blasters, but the neighborhood population was stable and
we had friendly, if brief, contacts with each other.

In 1973 the print shop acquired a binding machine; this made
it easier to publish larger books. During the next three years we printed
eleven books or pamphlets in addition to the bi-monthly *Radical
America*. We started by reprinting Rubin's *Essays* and Velli's
Manual.* Of the five B & R publications completed in 1974, only
one was originally written in English. This was *Wildcat! Dodge Truck,
June 1974*. The photos and texts were prepared by strike participants
and supporters, many of them activists around the *Fifth Estate*.

Before we could print Peter Arshinov's *History of the Makhnovist
Movement*, it had to be translated. Using the French translation and
a library copy of the Russian text, Fredy and I translated into English
the exploits of the Ukranian peasant leader whose partisans rallied
behind the anarchist black flag in their opposition to the "red"
Bolsheviks and the "white" defenders of the old order.†

Printing Voline's *The Unknown Revolution,* a book of 720 pages,
was a major undertaking. Most of it had been translated and published (in two volumes) by Freedom Press in London but it had been
out of print for some time. In the 1974 edition, two groups were listed
as co-publishers: Black & Red and Solidarity (Chicago). The mention of these two groups gives scant credit to the energies of more
than a dozen people who worked on this book. When *The Unknown
Revolution* appeared, Fredy felt that his views on the ideal use of
the print shop's resources had been vindicated as well as his principles on joint collaboration. As a publishing project, I think no other
book gave Fredy the satisfaction that Voline's book did; he saw this
project as a model of collective activity.

Fredy himself translated from French the pages omitted from
the first English edition. He also designed the cover and did the
printing. The layout, typesetting, proofreading and index were done
by our Chicago Solidarity friends, Ann Williams and Andy Tymowski,
and by their Oakland comrade, Dick Ellington. The enormous task
of collating, binding, trimming and packing was done by numerous

---

*The first printed copies of these two books were bound by hand. After sawing off
the back of the signatures, the pages were glued; the cover was attached in a later step.

†Our task was somewhat reduced by the prior translation into English of the pages
of Arshinov's book which Voline had quoted in *The Unknown Revolution.*

local and out-of-town friends. The summer of 1974 saw some congenial days when the print shop was filled with lively conversation — and diligent workers; there were festive evenings too, with food, drink and more discussions.

The two other works published that year were *Eclipse and Re-emergence of the Communist Movement* by J. Barrot and F. Martin; and *The Counter-Revolution in Ireland* by S. Van der Straeten and P. Daufouy. The latter was an article from *Les Temps Modernes,* which my sister, Ruth Nybakken, and I translated. Fredy and I typeset these two texts as well as Arshinov's book at night in a local graphic arts establishment where we paid an hourly rate for the use of their equipment.

In the 1970s, the designation "anarchist" came into increasing use when people referred to recent Black & Red books. Marxist analyses along the lines found in Rubin's *Essays* or in Fredy's *Reproduction* pamphlet were not pursued, and publishing two histories by anarchist authors about the Russian Revolution gave credence to the appellation. Our friends in Chicago had for some time identified their projects with the anarchist tradition, and Solzhenitsyn's *Gulag* books were very influential in making Fredy see political issues in terms of "the individual vs. the state." Fredy had, in fact, moved a long way from his views of the early 1960s, when he attentively followed United Nations proceedings and was far from antagonistic to prospects for a world government.

In this period Fredy read many accounts of the Spanish Revolution; events of these intense, critical years of extraordinary hopes and vile betrayal were made more vivid by Federico Arcos, a friend who, as a teenager, had participated in this struggle to escape the oppression imposed by banks, church and state. For Fredy, Franco and his army had always represented villainy in power and Fredy followed the example of the musician Pablo Casals and others who refused to go to Spain while the dictator ruled. Fredy never changed his evaluation of Franco, but with this reading of Spanish twentieth-century history, Fredy made some harsh judgments of Franco's adversaries: first, of the Republicans' Soviet allies; then, more painfully and with great outrage, of the anarchist leaders who had compromised their principles and accepted posts in the Spanish government.

In spite of Fredy's interest in and sympathy toward the anarchist tradition, at no time did he answer to the designation "anarchist"; he insisted that any label reduces the individual it is applied to. Earlier he had refused to answer to "Marxist" or "Situationist."

If the four Black & Red publications which appeared in 1975 fit into any single category, it would be "ultra-left" rather than "anarchist." Two of them severely criticize the practices of conventional labor organizations. *Lip and the Self-Managed Counter-Revolution,* an essay first published in the French journal *Négation,* depicts in an analytic and relatively cold light the attempts of employees at a French watch factory to take over the capitalist functions of a hard-pressed enterprise. *Unions Against Revolution* contains essays by G. Munis and John Zerzan documenting the role of labor unions as conservative, anti-liberatory commodity brokers. A series of pictures and quotes makes the same argument as the texts. The photo from 1973 shows "UAW organizers mobilizing goon squads to break a wildcat strike of militant workers at a Detroit plant," a new low for a union which prides itself on a militant past.

Maurice Brinton's *The Irrational in Politics* had originally been published by the libertarian London Solidarity group; it treats from a Reichean perspective themes similar to those found in Velli's *Manual.* Brinton attributes to childhood conditioning the individual's willingness to efface himself in order to further a supposedly "greater" cause.

The probing, sometimes eclectic, concerns of Jacques Camatte stimulated Fredy and other Chicago and Detroit dissidents trying to analyze — and ultimately to overturn — modern capitalist social relations. In *The Wandering of Humanity,* Camatte asserts that anthropomorphized Capital has always imposed and continues to impose its needs on human society, that many earlier movements associated with liberatory urges served to increase Capital's domination over human beings. Camatte reads history as an uninterrupted domestication of nature and human beings, and he includes revolutionary theory as a domesticating element: "After the domination of the body by the mind for more than two millennia, it is obvious that theory is still a manifestation of this domination."

For Camatte, "revolution [is] a project to reestablish community." The numerous individuals who worked to put Camatte's ideas into print saw their collective endeavor as a preliminary step toward establishing a community. We felt that our work at the print shop was an attempt to break down the barriers of specialized activity, first by working on all aspects of the project and then by doing it outside the framework of a commercial enterprise. In addition to the Detroit group of friends, Federico Arcos, Judy Campbell, the *Fifth Estate* circle, Marilyn and Jeff Gilbert, out-of-town friends — Peter Rachleff, Allan Foster, Geoff Hall — collaborated on the publications

printed in 1975 and discussed ways we could encourage and imple-
ment community.

Ten

Detroit's Jovial
Dissident Community

Fredy and I were part of a circle of lively individuals loosely
gathered around the *Fifth Estate*. These men and women were in no
way adherents of a party or platform, but we did hold similar views
about the indignities of wage labor, the pernicious effects of racism
in the U.S. and the unhealthy nature of a consumer society. Most
people in the group had jobs, but not professions. We identified with
drop-outs and scorned mainstream tastes and activities.

Rejecting middle-class conventions was not a wrenching choice
because the inner-city Cass Corridor area where most of the dissidents
lived was the center of Detroit's bohemian community. Many residents
of this area viewed the neighboring state institution, Wayne University, as an encroaching threat rather than a resource, and they made
efforts to organize cultural and self-help activities which they could
control. The food co-op and cinema club were undertakings which
had long histories. An auto co-op did not last as long, but its goals
to teach mechanical skills and to provide a service aided residents'
self-sufficiency. Local bands performed at street fairs and in neighborhood bars. There were frequent poetry readings and original theater
presentations. The Unitarian Church furnished meeting space for many
gatherings, both political and social. In the late 1970s, Ralph Franklin
and friends established another non-commercial space: the Grinning
Duck Club. The various locations of the *Fifth Estate* office were
always in the Cass Corridor area.

A permissive atmosphere prevailed in this part of midtown Detroit. Restrictive conventions were associated with the distant suburbs, while people committed to counter-cultural activities found mutual support among the residents of this area—students, drop-outs, artists, dissidents. The claim to "community" may have been exaggerated, but in this racially integrated neighborhood, there was tolerance for misfits, respect for those who preferred poverty to jobs, the recognition of a common bond that linked people one met, whether they were there by choice or necessity.

Detroit's radicals did not sit idle waiting for theoretical guidelines to appear in Black & Red publications. An institutional framework for radical activity was rejected long before any of us read either Brinton's essay on the leader principle or Camatte's *On Organization* or *The Wandering of Humanity*. A succinct two-word slogan characterized the position of *Fifth Estate* friends on this matter. Their "Fuck Authority!" posters and t-shirts were widely distributed. A number of audacious actions which put into practice the spirit of this motto preceded its appearance in 1975.

In the summer of 1973 Pat Halley publicly threw a pie in the face of a guru who claimed divine attributes. Pat's well-planned gesture received much media coverage, but it nearly cost him his life. One of the guru's disciples brutally attacked Pat and left him with a fractured skull; the man had come to Pat's home as a guest claiming he wanted to share his own critique of the guru.

The goals of career-oriented feminists and of *Ms.* magazine were debunked in a poster distributed by the *FE* at the end of 1974. The parody of the "feminist" position showed a tenant happily accepting eviction since it was done by women authorities; another woman proudly displayed the recognition plaque given her for superior shit-shovelling. Ironically condoning the State's torture apparatus as an acceptable tool for furthering a worthy cause, the poster carried to its logical conclusion the principle of using any and all means to assure success.

In the spring of 1974 an exhilarating evening of street theater took place in front of Cobo Hall, Detroit's convention center, where affluent civic leaders were assembling for a dinner. A hundred malcontents dressed as bums and wastrels gathered outside, lined up for the free soup (provided by the bums themselves), panhandled, sold pencils and distributed a pamphlet, "To Serve the Rich," which included recipes such as "Hearst Patties" and "Split Priest Soup."

One spring Sunday in 1975 found a poster affixed to a number of Detroit churches announcing "Christ's Body Found, Easter Cancelled."

Given the attitudes about consumption in the *FE* circle, an individual who acquired a new commodity often felt self-conscious and obliged to offer an explanation. But no one ever felt constrained to offer excuses for the consumption of food, even luxury food. We ate together frequently, sometimes in restaurants, more commonly in our homes. The pot-luck dinners—orgies of good food, laughter and conversation—were usually set up to commemorate an event or to introduce a visitor, but sometimes they were ad hoc gatherings.

The verbal prowess of the men in this group continually impressed Fredy. He listened with admiration—almost timidly—to their anecdotes, their succinct portrayals and devastating put-downs. But when theoretical issues were discussed, Fredy's historical analogies and logical reasoning captured everyone's attention. Fredy never considered himself skilled at repartee, but he knew he could characterize divergent viewpoints, show their origins and implications and convincingly articulate his position. Fredy used these gatherings of friends as a forum for expressing a synthesis of his current reading as well as his evolving insights. In addition to sharing their insights, his friends kept him up to date on events in Detroit and the world.

This circle of *Fifth Estate* friends has always had a unique genius. The choices made in one's daily activity, how one earns and spends money, are scrutinized closely. Over the years there were—and still are—heated arguments about recycling and consumption, about who to collaborate with on demonstrations, whether it is possible to use the mass media to communicate a radical perspective. Denunciations and defenses of spectator sports arouse passions. The principles involved in buying a luxury bicycle, handsome clothes, or a new car; the pros and cons of using electronic musical instruments, of copyrighting something one has written—these issues call into question everyone's practice and give rise to intense debates. Within the group, individuals are judged critically, but a sense of solidarity generally pervades even vociferous arguments. Support is always forthcoming when an individual acts as a rebel in an oppressive situation.

When there are out-of-town visitors—especially European ones—everyone makes great efforts to impress the guests with the group's integrity and wit. The setting of these festive pageants is Detroit, starting with the devastated part. Visitors are shown the abandoned buildings along the wide thoroughfares which extend for miles, thoroughfares where the main signs of life are other automobiles and an occasional party store. Europeans always insist that these areas look like war zones.

The guests also see the auto plants scattered around the city, many of them boarded up like so many other structures. Then, for contrast, there's a glimpse of an affluent suburb looking like the export version of the American lifestyle. And one of the city's few "gems" is on the itinerary: Belle Isle, the city park in the middle of the Detroit River.

The initiation continues on a more intimate level in the apartment or house of friends – in Detroit, but somewhat removed from the most blighted sections of the city. As people gather with food they have prepared, the conversation becomes animated. We are our own favorite audience and performers, but the presence of guests makes us aspire to new heights. Food and drink mellow the company; stories about local politicians, on-the-job sabotage, discrediting a bureaucrat or leftoid politico reinforce the impression that a joyful community can flourish in the midst of an American wasteland, that these inventive rebels will surely succeed in re-shaping society. Sometimes music and song further beguile those in attendance. Uninhibited attempts to speak the visitor's language add charm if not coherence.

I am obliged to use the present tense to write about this collective magic since a current victim of this enchantment, a visitor from West Germany, just asked me what I thought the selling price would be for a house displaying a "For Sale" sign down the street.

Food, drink and conversation were not the only pleasures that Fredy and I shared with *Fifth Estate* friends. There were outings to Point Pelee in Canada and to Michigan parks; we took bicycles, swim suits or cross country skis with us, depending on the season. Although Fredy was fifteen years older than many of these friends, it was a "community" of equals. He was attentive, but not condescending, toward views expressed by women; if he disagreed, he challenged them. Fredy was often light-hearted, willing to exchange silly stories. His cat imitations charmed all children and most adults. These were oral imitations but Fredy attributed his talent in this domain to certain other cat-like attributes he noted in his behavior.

When visitors came for a meal he bustled around the kitchen, happy to have company while he cooked, eager to share his recipes.

He was proud of his cooking skills and liked to be praised for the food he prepared.

Within the larger circle of friends there were some who were prone to anti-intellectualism. Fredy regarded as legitimate one aspect of this tendency—the urge to discredit authorities. In discussions, Fredy himself criticized severely many social theorists, but never on the grounds that an analysis was too complex, too complicated to grasp in an instant. He was intolerant of the unacknowledged and narrow criterion of some friends who grumbled about the difficulty of texts. These individuals found words they had learned before they were eighteen to be "acceptable" but words others had learned after they were eighteen to be "unacceptable."

Fredy put so much work into his writing projects he felt they were an extension of himself. He regarded endeavors of others accordingly and took care to follow and encourage his friends' creative projects, performances and exhibitions.

He sometimes found things to criticize in his friends' efforts. Fredy thought that theatrical works purporting to satirize a television program actually enhanced the authority of the media in general and the television personality in particular. Fredy held definite views about carelessness in printing projects. He thought sloppy writing, layout or printing, far from giving a personal touch to the words or images, suggested, minimally, indifference to the reader, and sometimes arrogance—as if the proffered words had such a magical, irresistible quality that the form chosen to present them was irrelevant.

He found it baffling that friends who found time to read the newspaper every day were unable to find time or unwilling to make the effort to read his books. Their lack of interest was all the more disappointing as Fredy felt his texts offered insights about issues that concerned his friends and were sometimes a synthesis of experiences they had in common.

Eleven

Letters of Insurgents

Fredy loved words, appreciated the diversity of languages, liked to mimic vocal patterns, to insert Serbian or French words into commonplace English expressions, to devise multi-lingual puns. His playful use of words appeared rarely in his writing, and then mainly in the choice of names for his characters.

Fredy was also awed by the power of words and knew his life had been deeply affected by thoughtful writers from his own and earlier eras. The shrinking arena for meaningful political activity in the early 1970s led Fredy to see himself less as an "activist" and more as a "rememberer." Fredy particularly wanted to "remember" the rebel, the individual who resisted the limitations imposed by his or her society. In *Letters of Insurgents,* his contribution to a history of the period in which he lived, he recorded various forms of rebellion; he was acquainted with many of them first-hand. He also recorded the dead ends, the co-optation and the thwarting of rebellious projects. The 830-page book, all words, was completed in 1976 and was a synthesis of most of Fredy's forty-two years; it follows fairly closely Fredy's physical and intellectual journeys, reporting the upheavals which had affected him, his family and his comrades in the middle third of the twentieth century.

Much of Fredy's own biography was given to Sophia, one of the correspondents, whose life was punctuated by peaks of enthusiasm and depths of disillusion as she repeatedly embraced a political/philosophic outlook and came to see its flaws. Sophia's first name denotes "wisdom," her last name is Nachalo, meaning "beginning," and despite her repeated disillusion with firmly-held tenets, she remains undaunted in her search for a new beginning.

By endowing certain characters in *Letters* with a fixed ideological perspective, Fredy evaluated many of his own and his contemporaries' philosophical and political tenets. Triumphant victorious armies who imposed the "people's will" on a subjugated population had never beguiled Fredy, but advocates of this form of "revolution"—fans of Castro, Ho, Mao, Lenin, among others—had long practiced their persuasive techniques on Fredy. Already in the 1950s he had rejected the possibility of enlightened statesmen charting global policies in the interest of all humans, and his critique of the desirability of such a leader holding the reins of power grew more focused and forceful. The villain of *Letters* is a humble bureaucrat who, believing he knows what is in his friends' best interests, assists them; a harmful, if not tragic, outcome is the inevitable result of his aid. Fredy's Yugoslav experience had discredited socialist planning from above and he caricatured its advocates in his account of Eastern European career-seeking. The brief sojourn in a university soured Fredy irrevocably toward that institution and his scorn for the system's ignominious mind-police pervades Sophia's account of her American experience.

The self-realization of the individual was a goal Fredy never repudiated, but in the post-1968 years he re-examined and discarded some of the approaches to self-realization that he had earlier considered acceptable. He came to view the Faustian urge as a fetter on self-realization since, at least in the twentieth century, it had served exclusively non-human ends. (The system with the ability to distort human impulses for its own purposes Fredy would later call "Leviathan.") This reappraisal was not easy; Fredy had been Faust's fellow-traveler for two decades. The analyses of the Frankfurt School writers helped him make the break; these readings also led him to question—and reject—many Enlightenment dogmas.

The continued search for an appropriate agency for social change is a basic theme of Fredy's historical novel. He examines labor unions and worker-managed industries and considers prospects for dropping out of society's mainstream. Fredy shared the impulses which led some of his contemporaries to try to find a niche where they could organize a living situation according to their own principles, but he concluded that it was not possible to escape from the dominant and coercive network. In *Letters* the urban counter-culture of illegal activities is depicted as exploitative and violent, although his descriptions of this milieu (based on minimal personal experience) have an aura of excitement. If Ted and Tina can be taken as characters their creator more or less approved of, one could say that in Fredy's view an individual has as good a chance for self-realization in an environment where stolen cars and prostitution predominate as in one where obedience and repressive morality prevail.

None of the characters in *Letters* finds an easy path to self-realization. Nor did Fredy; but in this tome which exalts communication between like-minded people, Fredy tells the reader that the hardships and anguish which come from accepting insurgency as a way of life are offset, first, by the sense of integrity one gains. Companionship and love, required elements in Fredy's conception of well-being, were further rewards Fredy believed the rebel could expect to find. The integrity, the love and companionship were made more profound by knowing of the bond, however tenuous, between one's "likes" in other places and in other times.

Fredy took seriously his role as "rememberer" of his fellow-rebels. This was the path he had chosen for his own self-realization.

In 1983, seven years after the appearance of *Letters of Insurgents*, Sophia Nachalo received an appreciative letter from a reader who lived in London. Like Sophia, the correspondent had been born in Eastern Europe and was trying to adjust insurgency to a new situation. Fredy was proud of his successful communication and responded to his reader with the following letter.

Dear Piri,

If *Letters of Insurgents* is the first "western" book which reflects some of yourself, you are the first person from "Magarna" who recognized herself (himself) in it and expressed this recognition. (Actually you're the second; a Yugoslav woman who lives in Paris preceded you by six years. And she wrote, a couple of years after the book's appearance, that the real "Yarostan," a worker in Subotica named Velimir Morača, had been re-arrested and had died in prison, probably murdered. He never saw the book.) Although the book was written before Velimir died, it was even at its inception intended as a remembrance, a type of monument, probably the only monument, to Jarostan (enragé) Vochek (čovek), to those who stayed and vanished and left no other trace except a memory in others. You surely knew Yarostan in Magarna (=anagram for Anagram). He was obviously not, as your essay makes clear, a member of the official opposition. Those people are the ones who survived, who learned to disguise and trim their integrity for the sake of their survival as Oppositionists. And we—Sophia and Sabina and you and I—are the ones who got out with nothing but fleeting memories of that integrity.

Yarostan was a "real" individual. The others are equally "real," but they are composites or fragments. Ted Nasibu (=Anubis, the Embalmer, preserver of the dead) was a fragment of me. For ten years I printed at a large cooperative print shop in Detroit, on equipment which was originally shared with forty or fifty other people (most of them professional "revolutionaries"). The Printing Co-op closed down in 1980, so that Ted no longer exists. I don't know what happened to his young friend Tina (=Faustina, Sabina's daughter). I suspect that Tina's friend, the Situationist, is a professor now. Tina's mother accidentally blew herself up with a bomb in 1969. (I still intend to tell the story of Sabina's death.) Sophia (myself) became something of a recluse after her sister's fatal accident, and an almost total recluse after the print shop closed. Black & Red still exists, but only as a postal box. . .; the printing is no longer done on cooperatively shared equipment.

Unlike Sophia, I was taken out of Czechoslovakia in 1939 (namely ten years earlier than she). Those in my family who stayed: grandmother, aunt and cousins, all vanished in concentration camps. Like Sophia, I did not derive any personal meanings from my experience until I was a university student, by which time the language of camp guards was Russian and English, not German. I did not have an exchange of long letters with a childhood comrade, because I had been too young and no comrades had survived. I actually re-visited by birthplace (in the early 1960s), but I was not allowed to remain; only Yugoslavia gave me an extended visa. I lived in Beograd for over three years. I met Velimir soon after his release from twelve years in Communist labor camps, "self-managed" ones at that. (Your dream of the waterless pool and the "voluntary suicides" is a perfect description of the "self-managed" camp.) I met others: Russians, Czechs, Hungarians. The disappearance of my aunts and cousins became meaningful to me, but in Sophia's form, not my own. I did not focus on my own early experience until later, responding to present-day pogromists who perpetrate their ugly deeds in the name of my dead cousins. So it seems that Nachalo was a Beginning, not for Sophia but for me, and when I was at last able to start with the beginning, my own, I signed my own name.

　. . .

I was deeply moved by your responses to the *Letters.* Thank you for sharing them.

Fredy Perlman

Twelve

Music

*— The only -ist name I
respond to is "cellist."*

Soon after coming to Detroit, Fredy took up the cello. He had played on a borrowed instrument briefly in New York City but in 1972, at 38, he was essentially a beginner. His goal was to play classical chamber music, an activity to which I had always been devoted. Fredy took occasional lessons but was too impatient to follow the conventional pedagogic methods. He practiced music his teachers considered too hard for him and he learned vibrato long before he was "ready" for it. He had nicely shaped hands for cello-playing but his motor skills weren't remarkable. In the beginning, he complained about how hard it was for his left hand to make vertical motions while his right hand made horizontal ones.

Fredy's success in becoming a cellist was due to considerable natural talent, to his familiarity with classical music (as an elementary school student in Cochabamba, Bolivia he had won a contest to identify a number of standard orchestral works) and to his exceptional determination. Although in later years he spent more time practicing the cello (up to two hours a day), even in the beginning he could concentrate on a difficulty with persistence and intensity.

During the late 1970s, as the number of Fredy's collective political projects declined, he increasingly took part in the chamber music sessions of amateur musicians in the Detroit area. He found himself associating with middle-class Americans who were well-established professionally, some of them even religious or patriotic. Fredy observed that etiquette in this circle frowned on ideological discussions. When a new player presented himself or herself, it was acceptable to inquire about the player's general social activity, but controversial non-musical subjects were avoided. Fredy's occasional provocative statement usually met with silence. This disappointed him, but he came to comply with the group's standards: prestige and popularity were in direct proportion to one's playing abilities. Even possession of a valuable instrument was no guarantee of acceptance.

Fredy found enormous gratification in the music sessions. He was pleased to be accepted as an equal by people who had been playing for decades and he was elated by the music-making. He nevertheless formulated a political defense of his new activity, asserting that chamber musicians' self-organization was one of the rare examples in contemporary society where people initiated a non-lucrative activity outside an institutional framework.

Fredy's appreciation of the chamber musicians was not unequivocal, however. A few he found intellectually lazy; others painfully oblivious of the world around them. And a single individual might exhibit these negative qualities alongside breathtaking musicianship. Fredy created one such character in Book Two of *The Strait,* a woman whose mindless remarks and reproachable actions were forgiven when she began playing the piano.

As his proficiency grew, Fredy expanded the size of his musical groups and in January 1983 he joined the Dearborn Orchestra. He prepared for the weekly rehearsals by practicing with a taped recording of the selections chosen for the performance. At the orchestra concerts Fredy was obliged to wear a suit and a tie. He also wore these music clothes when we were hired to play quartet music at weddings or dinners. Fredy saw these jobs as an acknowledgement of his musical skills and never objected to exchanging them for money (as he did with vehemence when writing skills were in question).

Almost every August, starting in 1973, Fredy and I went to Interlochen, Michigan for a week of institutionally organized chamber music. Fredy was charmed by the suspension of conventional signs of social prestige: one's profession, income and automobile were matters of indifference. The two hundred musicians—mostly middle-aged or older—lived in dormitory rooms and docilely lined up for the institutional food served on metal trays. A unifying bond linked these people who had come to northern Michigan to live intensely for a week. Many unabashedly indulged youthful impulses. What counted here was technique and musicality in, for example, "opus

18, number 6." (In these circles it was superfluous to name the composer.)

The institutional aspects of the adult music camp did not charm Fredy. Faculty and staff wore clothes which identified their status, participants were given a badge which told their name and instrument and which was required for entrance to concerts; the color scheme of this "National Music Camp's" auditorium was red, white and blue. Fredy tried to apply the word "fascist" to the mentality of the camp's administrators, but since so many of the rules went unobserved by the adult musicians, he did not insist on its appropriateness. "Authoritarian" and "arbitrary" were terms that some of the other players accepted when complaining that assignment into groups was determined by unchallengeable ratings. After the 1984 session (his last) Fredy wrote an open letter in which he outlined his objections to the system of classification. He sent it to a dozen or more players who he thought shared his attitudes. Only two responded, and they were non-committal; none was eager to agitate for change.

Fredy mellowed during the years he made music. His indignation over social ills did not cease, nor did his denunciations against nationalism and racism lose their fire, but he judged less harshly the individuals with whom he came in contact. He came to have a more tolerant view of persons he would have rejected twenty years earlier. His increased tolerance can be seen in his last work, *The Strait,* where characters from a wide political spectrum are sympathetically depicted and their choices—even ones Fredy thought unwise—treated with understanding. One character, Shabeni, in 1800, after a tribal dance in l'Arbre Croche on the shore of Lake Michigan, told the book's narrator

> he was ashamed of the crosses and the names [of those his people denounced as enemies], but not of the dance itself. He told us the dance came from the world described on our grandmother's scroll, and that his kin would remain Rootkin so long as they continued to dance, even if they named their own kin enemies and the Invaders saviors. When they forget the dance as well, he said, they'll die. [p. 271]

Shabeni was a spokesman for very few of Fredy's views, but the two agreed on this point: dancing—and music-making—nourish elements precious to human experience. It saddened Fredy to see spectators and auditors renounce personal participation for vicarious enjoyment.

Thirteen

Health

When he was 23, Fredy told me that he didn't expect to live beyond 30. It was a statement he recalled occasionally, the last time in August 1984 when he turned 50. Then he felt smug, as if he had somehow overcome an evil charm put on him by childhood doctors. In Bolivia, one of the doctors asserted that Fredy's heart valve had been seriously damaged by rheumatic fever and warned that the ten-year-old Fredy should expect to spend most of his life in bed, that walking would endanger his health and running would kill him.

Fredy took seriously the doctor's diagnosis, but disregarded the admonition (except for running). Fredy's self-image was one of a borderline invalid even though, until he was fifty, his heart condition caused him almost no physical discomfort. He did suffer from headaches and stomach pains, sometimes severe enough to make him go to a hospital emergency room. He never found a cure for these ailments. In his 40s, he made some changes in his diet, eliminating the two quarts of milk he customarily drank each day; at this time he also substituted large quantities of tea for large quantities of coffee. He refused to see cigarettes as having harmful effects on his aches and pains and he continued smoking thirty to forty cigarettes a day.

He later made some changes in his smoking habits: following Kemal Orcan's example, Fredy started rolling his own cigarettes. Pulling the tobacco, homemade filters and the bamboo rolling device out of his leather pouch, he made the creation of the cigarette part of the smoking ritual. His tobacco consumption did diminish in his last years. He refrained from smoking in the homes of certain friends. Only slightly responsive to the growing antagonism to smoking, he insisted that the official government campaign against smoking was dishonest manipulation. He maintained that risks from tobacco were minimal compared to the massive pollution from industrial sources. Besides the satisfaction he got from smoking, Fredy associated tobacco with this continent's indigenous people and, in his view, its origin enhanced its value.

During the first thirteen years I knew him, Fredy never consulted a doctor. In Detroit, he made some effort to find the cause of his stomach aches and grudgingly agreed to have his heart condition monitored.

The first cardiologist he saw wanted him to go from the examining room to a neighborhood Detroit hospital for a catheterization and from there to heart surgery. This heart specialist told him he could drop dead just sitting there; he warned that for someone in Fredy's condition, the time required to get a second opinion could jeopardize his life. In those days, Fredy's medical bills were paid by the state's social services agency, and the doctor's financial motives were naturally suspect. Nevertheless, Fredy was alarmed. The second opinion was reassuring: no surgery just yet, but the prospect of heart surgery became a future possibility.

Five years later, in 1976, a surgeon at Henry Ford Hospital convinced Fredy of the need to replace the aortic valve and Fredy submitted to open heart surgery. The experience was terrifying and painful. During his convalescence, Fredy said he would never endure heart surgery again.

The operation gave Fredy some peace of mind, although it in no way increased his vigor. The pig's valve which was substituted for his defective one was expected to function for five years. Thus the need for another surgery was built in to the initial one. Fredy had rejected the alternative of a non-organic valve replacement because the plastic and metal device would have required him to take daily doses of anti-coagulant medication.

Fredy vacillated on the question whether the heart surgery had extended or even enhanced his life. Sometimes he felt that he had been merely a gullible consumer of the medical industry's expertise.

Until a few months before his death, Fredy carried on his very active routine. He shovelled snow (slowly, to be sure), gardened, carried heavy boxes of books, bicycled, went cross-country skiing, swam, did house repairs. He ate heartily, but didn't gain weight.

In late 1984 or early 1985, he became aware of a physical decline. There were more frequent dizzy spells, he felt the need for an after-

noon nap, his pounding heart would wake him at night, he was reluc-
tant to climb two flights of stairs.

In the spring of 1985 Fredy consulted a number of doctors,
surgeons and cardiologists. All the reports were alarming. In addition to an uneven heartbeat, one examination revealed a large
abdominal aneurysm.

The surgeon who had performed the 1976 operation advised
another one. It was scheduled for late June, but was cancelled when
catheterization showed that Fredy's heart was significantly weaker
than in 1976 and that the mitral valve, too, was malfunctioning. The
risk of surgery would be considerably greater. The doctor wanted
to reconsider.

Fredy did not seriously reconsider his decision to have surgery.
Although the doctors never promised a magical cure, Fredy believed
the replaced valves would permit him to continue a normal life. His
skepticism about the skills of the medical profession was more than
counterbalanced by his fear of being an invalid. The prospect of a
debilitating stroke or heart attack followed by the "medical police's"
constant surveillance led him to choose the drastic alternative.

In the last month of his life, Fredy continued to work on *The
Strait,* but health problems preoccupied him. He consulted all friends
connected with the medical profession. Our many visitors were told
about his situation, the alternatives described. Fredy did not ask us
to decide if he should have heart surgery, but he did ask us if we
had arguments against the surgery. No one tried to talk him out of
going through with it. The surgeon said the risk was 20%, four chances
out of five did not seem too hazardous to most of us.* The second
week in July, Fredy called Dr. Magilligan to say he wanted the surgery
scheduled before Magilligan left on vacation in August.

Once the decision was made, Fredy continued his projects, spent
time with friends, went on a short camping trip to Stratford and Lake
Huron, mailed out a new Black & Red publication, played chamber
music. The morning of the surgery itself, July 26, 1985, preparing
to climb on the cart that wheeled him away, Fredy reminded me of
minor tasks we had left unfinished.

Later that day, after the surgeon had replaced both the mitral
and aortic valves, Fredy's heart was unable to resume its functioning.

*My view, based on the surgeon's reluctance to operate in June as well as the tragic
outcome, is that the risk was significantly underestimated; but Fredy was so distressed
about his failing health that I think the statistical numbers played a very small part in his
decision.

Fourteen

"Who's Zarelli?"

Fredy completed the manuscript of *Letters of Insurgents* before his first heart surgery in May of 1976. During his convalescence we typeset and prepared it for printing.* Through anarchist friends in Toronto, we made contact with a worker-run graphic arts enterprise in Kitchener, Ontario. The hospitable group of worker-activists who operated Dumont Press Graphix welcomed us, taught us and housed us during various periods of the summer and fall of 1976.

Fredy and I learned to type "blind" on machines which punched paper tapes; the tapes were then fed into a Merganthaler VIP computer-photo compositor. We worked at night when the machines were available for non-commercial projects. More than once, a typo on the paper tape instructed the VIP to do weird things, sometimes to erase its "memory." Patient, smiling Steve Izma and his Dumont collaborators rescued us from despair when things went wrong.

Fredy was never fascinated by or enamored of the sophisticated equipment we used in Kitchener. He wanted Black & Red publications to be readable and visually attractive. To accomplish this he was willing to learn how to operate the machines. He was aware that, far from being master of these machines, he had to conform to the requirements imposed by their logic. Fredy's gratitude toward Dumont was directed to the individuals who maintained the premises and equipment, not toward the machines.

---

*Millard Berry composed an excellent cover by juxtaposing pictures of two friends on his photo of the Detroit skyline shortly before it became dominated by the intimidating Renaissance Center towers.

At the time of his 1976 surgery Fredy received a copy of Ivan Illich's *Medical Nemesis* from friends. This searing critique of contemporary medical practices was one Fredy found all too accurate, and after reading the book, he bought a copy to give to Magilligan, the cardiac surgeon. This was a symbolic gesture since Fredy knew that a meaningful reform of the medical profession was unlikely to originate in the upper echelons of its hierarchy.

In the months following his surgery, Fredy and many friends prepared a theatrical work which debunked the practices of individual health practitioners and the sacrosanct medical establishment itself. All the collaborators had had first-hand experience—either as professional health workers or as victims. There was a wealth of material.

Greedy physicians and repressed female administrators were not the only types depicted in the sequence of twenty-four scenes set in a large metropolitan hospital. A well-intentioned woman doctor who truly believed in her work was an inadvertent villain (much like Titus Zabran in *Letters of Insurgents*). Her name was Dr. DeAth (pronounced Dee Ath).

The title of the piece, "Who's Zarelli?" came from a reference to a lost or misplaced patient. Although the underlying theme was decidedly serious, most scenes were humorous exaggerations of real experiences. Two performances of the play were given at Easy Space in May 1977.

Fredy enjoyed and was stimulated by the frequent meetings and rehearsals for "Who's Zarelli?" Over twenty people took part in it, many volunteering technical skills. It was a collective effort, carried out without authorities; decisions were made by consensus.

Fredy found the experience enormously frustrating too. Some people took their commitment much more lightly than he did: they were late to or absent from rehearsals, they failed to learn their lines, they forgot about a task they had promised to do. Fredy understood that self-organized activities are supposed to be free of coercion and hoped that a personal obligation to the project and the group would motivate his friends to honor their commitments. He never hesitated to express his indignation at the offhand promises made and then forgotten by his collaborators, but he rarely attributed them to malicious intent. Rather, he accused these friends of discrediting an activity which was attempting to transcend the usual way projects are organized in this society.

In a typewritten sheet that he circulated a couple days before the performance, Fredy objected to two specific aspects of the nearly-completed project that disappointed him.

—Various last minute requests (written down so as not to waste everyone's time in a long discussion)

People adding stunts and gags at the last minute: Could you please think them through first and decide if they belong in a play depicting the routine (of inhumanity and crime) of a *hospital ward*? For example, painting a ward with patients in it, fumigating patients with roach spray, a patient having and waving a rifle in a hospital ward—are funny gags. But these acts have no truth in them as acts that take place "routinely" in a hospital. In my opinion, the entire play is only as true as its grossest exaggeration; if some acts are lies, all the acts are reduced to lies. This is unfortunate because the central theme of the play, the fact that human beings are destroyed by the medical establishment, is the "truth" the play was trying to depict—but this theme can be no truer than the degree of truth supported by the rest of the play.

The end of act I (before the intermission): it is the end of Jones's first day in the hospital. A conversation ends (Jones and DeAth). The repressive character of total medical care is raised as a question (Floyd). A visitor comes looking for a patient misplaced by the hospital bureaucracy (Zarelli). The routine goes on (the noise pollution: Splitgerber and his TV, the pagings, beeps, phones, etc.). The act ends.

My problem is that I don't see how several new elements contribute to this scene: namely the sudden running and banging, the dying fumigator, Splitgerber's waving of the gun, etc. This may all stimulate laughs (silliness often does) but I think it's dumb, and to me it's a disappointing end to scenes worked out over a two or three month period in a totally different spirit.

. . .

Sound and Light: The difference between night and day was to be depicted in the original conception: the noise pollution of the day, the sleep-destroying tension of the night. Initially this difference was to be created "amateurishly" by means of clock, hall lights, TV lights and sounds, ward lights, bedside lamps, nurse's station lights. Since there's no curtain, sound and light effects were also to denote scene changes (passage of hours or days), simultaneously illustrating the dehumanizing character of the electronic communication (the constant pagings) and the "cultural" propaganda (the TV programs). "Amateurish" devices to do this were set up two weeks ago because those who had said they'd do this hadn't started yet. At the last minute this setup was supplanted, but ever since the "amateur" setup was supplanted by "professional" effects, I haven't been able to distinguish day from night, or to notice lapses of time, or the dehumanizing character of the institutional communication. I feel this as another loss, and I request that those responsible for it try to restore at least a minimum of the original intention.

Finally, I think everyone in the play has enriched it immensely with marvelous depictions of characters and ingenious satirical acts—but these will be communicated only if we support each other by remembering our lines and cues.

Fredy

Hughthir White reminded me, in 1988, that Fredy's verbal formulation of his argument against the slapstick routines was: "If audience laughter is your goal, there's an infallible way to get it. Just piss on yourself. They'll laugh." But neither Fredy's verbal nor written objections succeeded in eliminating the slapstick routines from the performances. The lack of coherence in the presentation bothered Fredy; the fact that it seemed to bother his collaborators so little angered him. He felt that their tolerance for last-minute changes resulted in a haphazard production and represented a fundamental change in the original project. In his view there had been a well-defined perspective when they began the project. He was disappointed and frustrated that he alone was arguing to retain it.

Fredy's clearly-articulated anti-authoritarian principles kept him from urging his view on the basis of greater experience or knowledge (which in any case would have been rejected by this group of fiercely autonomous individuals) and he knew that ingrained habits made it hard to achieve new work relations, but his confidence in a consensus approach to collective projects was shaken by the fact that the "rightness" of his cause was not recognized by people he thought agreed with the principles he was advocating with such fervor. Some individuals may have hesitated to champion Fredy's suggestions because they were not eager to be a spokesperson for another's point of view. Fredy was at least ten years older than most of the friends working on "Who's Zarelli?" Although he took great care to avoid speaking as an authority, some may have seen him as the man who was trying to "run the show." It is possible that certain individuals chafed under Fredy's intense verbal formulations and were satisfied to see the project move in a direction contrary to Fredy's. Whatever the explanation, Fredy's logical arguments and vigorous formulations won him few allies.

Fredy's anger toward fellow participants did not endure once the project came to an end. When remembering it, he concentrated on the gratification "Who's Zarelli?" had provided. But Fredy never again took part in a non-institutional project involving many people. He always insisted that a non-authoritarian approach was indispensable in order to achieve collective goals, but after 1977 he consciously chose activities which would depend less crucially on his friends' collaboration.

Fifteen

The Project of Writing
an Epic of the
World-Changers' Epoch

In May 1977, two days after the final performance of "Who's Zarelli?" Fredy and I left for a month-long trip to Europe. We spent three weeks in France, one week in London. This was our first visit to Europe in eight years.

We were welcomed by our many friends in Paris and joined three of them, Ghislaine and Maurice Fhima and Michèle Bloch on a trip by car to central and southern France. In Brignoles we met Jacques Camatte who housed and feasted us. The superb meal Camatte prepared for us was not the only memorable *provençal* meal associated with this trip. Before returning to Paris, the five of us ate a *bouillabaisse* in a restaurant in a seacoast town on the Mediterranean. The ritual enacted by the restaurant personnel made us feel we had roles in a theater piece. The "show" lasted for three hours; we laughed and enjoyed the setting as we savored the numerous courses.

Fredy was never a passive tourist, waiting for someone to show him the sights. Having had such visitors, he took care to avoid that dependency. On the contrary, in an effort to stimulate our hosts and friends in other cities, Fredy often "performed." He was prepared to give a coherent account of, for example, life in Detroit or the Left in the United States. In discussions during the 1977 trip, he defended his views on the nefarious effects of technology. Like Fredy, our

European friends had been deeply affected by the events of May 1968 and had made a break with a "workerist" perspective, but few agreed with Fredy's all-inclusive critique of machines and of modern agriculture. Maurice protested that the abolition of machines in agriculture would necessarily imply a return to the digging stick, that any intermediate technology would inevitably lead to a mechanization comparable to the one in effect today. Fredy did not challenge Maurice's conclusion, but steadfastly asserted his belief that it was impossible for societies in which mining and factories play a significant role to be healthy and human-oriented.

Fredy offered no program for getting rid of the polluting commodities but did not shrink from the implications of his position. When someone protested that what Fredy advocated would rule out automobiles, buses and airplanes ("and you *did* come here on an airplane, didn't you? How can you be so ungrateful for the travel possibilities industrialism offers?"), Fredy replied, "We—and everyone on the planet—would be better off without them. Meaningful lives are more likely without continent-hopping."

Fredy retained central aspects of Marx's thought: he saw all factory-made objects as the embodiment of the regimented energy of the individuals that created them. Unlike Marx, Fredy found the regimentation unacceptable and this led him to repudiate the objects themselves. The commodities emerging from industrial society's rationalized production lines now seemed to Fredy to be detrimental to human well-being. The majority of these products serve the needs of other machines, not human needs. Fundamental natural relationships are disrupted and Mother Earth is despoiled in the process.

This sweeping critique of machines did not come to him entirely from theoretical sources. For some time, Fredy had referred to the binding machine in the print shop as "a capitalist machine." The human price exacted for its services was a high one: it imposed its own rhythm, the piercing shriek of the saw was hard to endure, the potential dangers of the gears, saw and hot glue were hardly trivial for the operators.

In a context where manufactured commodities are seen as impediments to a healthy interaction between individuals and between an individual and the natural environment, a call for "full employment," for "the right to a job," for "wages for housework" is misguided, at best. Fredy agreed with Camatte that the demand that everyone be a wage worker was evidence that we are living in the epoch of "the *real* domination of Capital" and that the slogans were "the voice of Capital." Fredy thought Camatte's description of labor unions as "rackets" was apt.

The increasing disapproval Fredy expressed toward the plethora of manufactured products in contemporary society resulted, at least in part, from his growing appreciation for earlier cultures. Fredy never selected a specific single epoch as a model for humans to resurrect, but the richness and variety of earlier societal relationships made him see the current system as just one of many possibilities.

In 1976 Fredy undertook a systematic study of world history. He started by reading the volumes of the *Cambridge Ancient History* series. During the next five years he compiled a forty-page list of books he wanted to read. It was organized into categories like "Early modern Europe," "North American Archaeology," "Science and Technology," "Islam." These lists contained works of fiction as well as historical and cultural studies. Fredy took notes from many of the books on this list, sometimes typing out extensive passages. To help organize all the material, he prepared large sheets (the size of a table top) on which he recorded events according to chronology and continent. These charts begin with 9000 B.C. and continue to the present. Some of the column headings are: "Social Relations" which is subdivided into "Rural" and "Urban"; "Capital"; "Material Conditions (Technology)"; "Literature." He used several colors of ink to record the entries. This survey of world history covers at least eighty large sheets, some filled with minuscule handwriting. On sheets equally large, but less numerous, he made charts of the history of art and architecture. Picture post cards and other graphic illustrations from a particular era are included as visual documentation.*

The study of ancient cultures gave Fredy a strong incentive to visit the sites where the events he read about had taken place. Between 1978 and 1983 we traveled extensively in North America and made a two-month visit to eastern Mediterranean countries. Fredy planned the itinerary for these trips to include places of historical interest.

To prepare for the autumn 1978 trip to Turkey, Syria, Egypt and Greece, Fredy started in the spring to study Turkish, Arabic and Greek. Kemal Orcan gave him a lot of help with the Turkish language. Kemal, too, was fascinated by the varied cultures that had existed in the vicinity of his birthplace, Iskenderun, and for long hours he and Fredy would discuss the books they were reading and speculate about possible implications of the ancient ways for modern society.

*Some of Fredy's early reminders to himself about note-taking and charts are reproduced in the Appendix, page 151.

Kemal's thoughtful description of village life in Turkey prepared us to like the people we met there, but hardly prepared us for the prodigious hospitality that was showered on us. The generosity of people who were expecting us was not so surprising; it was the several chance acquaintances who gave unstintingly of their time and refreshments (and even housing, in one village) that made us feel humble. To these welcoming people we were guests, not tourists. The Turkish hospitality — which contrasts favorably with the more indifferent American version — impressed us because it was so obviously genuine, uncalculating. (In Egypt we experienced calculated hospitality at various times: once involving an invitation to a meal in the home of a young man; more commonly, the expectation that an answer to questions like "Where is the toilet?" warranted monetary recompense.)

Turks were delighted that we tried to speak their language. Fredy had mastered it to the extent that he could successfully ask directions, get us rooms. Fredy's apparent fluency resulted in some of the responses being much too complicated, but we tried to catch key phrases like "Turn left at the second street."

In one village we attended a wedding celebration where the guests were segregated according to sex. The women welcomed me and offered the delicious food, but without Fredy, communication was more by gesture than with words. Two weeks later we arrived on foot in a village in a wine-producing region. On this Saturday the residents were celebrating the grape harvest and we were invited to join the festivities. We followed the crowd to a riverbank picnic area where wine was plentiful and savored by all those attending (an untypical occurrence to judge by what we saw elsewhere in Turkey).

In this, our first visit to Asia, we were awed by the richness and variety of cultures. Ottoman and Seljuk mosques, Hellenic ruins and prehistoric urban sites all helped us to visualize at least the physical setting where earlier residents had led their lives. We found our way to the sites by bus, by taxi or on foot. There were few Turkish or foreign tourists. Often we were alone. Sometimes everyday life quaintly intruded on the momentous historical visit — as when the taxi driver who took us to Çatal Hüyük (to see the remains of the oldest known city) stopped on the way to pick two watermelons from a field along the road. One was for us, one for him.

From Turkey we had hoped to go to Iraq, but the embassy officials in Ankara thrust our American passports back at us through the gate with a resounding "No!" There was no opportunity for pleading. This refusal served to corroborate Fredy's bitter assessment that, with each generation, travel becomes more and more restricted.

After a three-day stay in Syria where we went by bus across the desert to visit Palmyra (formerly a glittering city-state and desert oasis situated on the overland trading route), we continued on to Egypt.

The artistic and architectural wonders stretching along both sides of the Nile were clearly creations of an "affluent society," the ancient prosperity contrasting sharply with conditions in contemporary Egypt. We tried to explain the seeming indifference of present-day inhabitants to the artifacts and structures that surround them and wondered if it was because neither of the two rival religions—Coptic Christianity and Islam—incorporates the ancient Egyptian heritage into their religious tradition. One factor was certainly the Egyptians' resentment of the wealth of foreign tourists and the visitors' sole interest in museum people.

Fredy and I did not enjoy being classed with the standard Western European tourists and we tried to speak Serbo-Croatian to each other when we were in public. The numerous hustlers guessed we were English-speaking and they were skeptical when we answered the opening question of their appeal, "Where do you come from?" with "Yugoslavia." Fredy's attempts to communicate in Arabic were always repulsed.

In late 1977 Fredy started an outline for a history of "the world-changers."* The form of the intended story was fundamentally changed more than once, but the desire to understand and record in a narrative the conquests of the European Invaders as well as the resistance they encountered structured Fredy's reading and traveling during his last decade.

Many of the North American sites we visited figure in the pages of the work which emerged from his study. The majority are drastically different from the days when Obenabi, the narrator of Fredy's epic, inhabited the region; but some, like Gnadenhuten in Ohio and New Harmony in Indiana, are maintained as museums. A small number of Rootkin mounds still remain (in areas now designated as West Virginia; Cahokia, Illinois; southern Ohio). Others can be found near the Iowa cliffs overlooking the Mississippi, in Michigan near Grand Rapids and in Detroit.

In 1979 Fredy and I visited museums and sites of historical interest in Ontario, Illinois, Indiana and southern Ohio. We also made

*Four pages of Fredy's early notes are reproduced in the Appendix on pages 151-154.

a trip to see the "stonelodges" and "earthlodges" of Obenabi's distant kin in Oklahoma, New Mexico and Arizona. In other years we went on camping trips around Michigan. We got acquainted with the Upper Peninsula, the shores of Lake Michigan and Lake Huron, spent time in and around l'Arbre Croche ("the leaning tree village") where Obenabi had two of his visions.

In his epic Fredy managed to include subtle references even to locales inhabited by the early Mayans. We visited many of them — Tikal, Chichen Itza, Palenque and Copan — during the first three weeks of 1980 when we went to Guatemala, Honduras and the Yucatan.

In the early 1980s we also made trips to New England, eastern New York and the region around the Outer Banks on the Carolina coast. Traces of the original people are faint in this part of the continent, but many well-stocked museums provide extensive exhibits of artifacts. Fredy was an avid viewer of these collections but his approbation was matched by his antagonism to this type of historical museum. He observed that the seemingly philanthropic individuals, the donors of large collections, aware that a unique culture was dying and concerned to preserve a record of it, were often personally responsible for conditions which made it impossible for this culture to exist. In Fredy's eyes, the fact that Henry Schoolcraft, Lewis Cass (agents of the U.S. government in the Michigan territories) and their likes preserved some of their victims' cultural artifacts did not diminish their villainy. Containing, as they do, the spoils of war between cultures, Fredy saw these museums as tributes to the victors.

In a text written in 1983 Fredy berates "trophy-hunters called Archaeologists" and in his last (as yet unpublished) book, he denounces the distortions characteristic of many anthropology students who analyze a culture about to be eliminated. He asserts that their interest and appreciation are rooted in a sense of their own racial and cultural superiority. The conclusions of these "students" uncannily find a way of arrogating to their own culture achievements they are unable to ignore.

> The large, baby-faced man called Loos-gas...spoke of his encounters with extensive earthworks in the Beautiful Valley, on the shores of the Wabash and on the Strait itself; he spoke as if he were displaying a collection of coins or trophies. He did not ask any questions of Wabnokwe, nor did he address himself to her, but to the room itself. He said he had encountered all those earthworks in places that were empty of human

inhabitants or places recently vacated by temporary inhabitants. The builders of those earthworks, he said, had vanished, leaving no traces other than the mounds themselves. What mysterious, vanished peoples had built those mounds? he asked.

Angered by the self-assurance with which the man made his arbitrary assertions, Wabnokwe said she knew of no mystery; the mound builders had been the ancestors of the villagers exterminated by governor Loos-gas and his armies. She even offered to introduce him to the living mound builders who, until just before the war, had buried their dead in the mound by the spring behind neighbor Wit-nags' house.

The governor's round face turned pale with rage, yet he spoke softly, as if addressing a child. Men of science, he said, distinguish fact from hearsay. Science, he said, is not a collection of superstitions. Extensive earthworks, he said, required architects and engineers; they could not have been raised by the miserable savages his armies had pacified and moved. Ancient Huns, he said, or Vikings, or even Jews, had been capable of building such extensive earthworks. His voice grew louder as he began to expound the scientific theories that accounted for such evidences of civilization in a sea of barbarism, . . . Wabnokwe knew he had not come to ask, but to tell; his eyes and his ears were mere decorations; it was with his science that he saw and heard, and this organ had told him, long before he had encountered any earthworks, that his near or distant ancestors were the only people capable of building them. Wabnokwe backed out of the salon . . . ; she heard the powerful voice say "We" several times; she knew that "We" included only Loos-gas, Jay-may and Wit-nags; "We" meant "We white men"; "We" were the mound builders.

Fredy revised his story of the world-changers as a result of his travels. *The Strait,* the epic which emerged, commemorated the end of an epoch, as planned, but the "end" was moved from the mid-twentieth century to the middle of the nineteenth. Too neutral a term, "world-changers" became "world-destroyers." Sabellicus-Faust-Alberts, originally to be one of the epic's two central characters, does not appear in *The Strait,* at least not as a personification of the Western spirit. By the time he came to write it, Fredy apparently found the Faustian qualities too unredeeming even to construct a character around them. The voracious, enterprising drive is spread among several historical figures: Winamek, Ou-shn-tn, Boatmaker, Loos-gas.

Similarly, the forms of rebellion which Sabina, the other principal character, was to have practiced, were given to numerous other characters, some historical, others Fredy's own creation (Mendideti, Dehenyante). Many of Sabina's qualities *do* remain embodied, however, in Obenabi's sister Wabnokwe, whose name means Dawn, Rising Sun, Easterner. Wabnokwe was a child of the Enlightenment and remained loyal to its precepts until she could no longer deny the tragic devastation inherent to its practices.

Fredy had used the coming to self-awareness as a dramatic technique in earlier works (*Plunder, Letters of Insurgents*); in *The Strait*, Wabnokwe's disenchantment and break with her Enlightenment mentors parallel a trajectory that Fredy had himself followed. He made Wabnokwe an accomplished cellist and an individual who, seeking social harmony, believed it could be achieved by rational means. The events of Wabnokwe's life (1791 to 1841) disabused her of this faith. Though he did not live them personally, they had the same effect on Fredy.

Two nineteenth century American authors, Hawthorne and Melville, helped Fredy to see the gulf between Rootkin and Invader, and to see that the latter's jealous demand for dominance precluded any possibility to live in harmony. Melville's sinister, indefatigable, many-faceted Confidence Man depicted the nineteenth century New World version of the arrogant spirit which the Frankfurt School writers analyzed more abstractly in the twentieth century. Fredy saw in historian Arnold Toynbee one of his contemporaries who painfully — but honestly — reevaluated earlier views; he was deeply moved by Toynbee's book, *Mankind and Mother Earth,* in which the historian's Christian outlook was largely abandoned. At the end of Book Two of *The Strait,* Liket, an important and sympathetic character, undergoes a similar conversion when her lifelong effort to communicate a generous, universalist Christian message to the guileless people whom she teaches in Detroit and in l'Arbre Croche is thwarted by racist life-destroyers who claim her Jesus as their god.

Readings in anthropology, especially those of Marshall Sahlins and Pierre Clastres, made Fredy reject as ideological blindness Hobbes's generally accepted dictum about the short and brutish nature of life in prehistorical societies. Fredy's "primitivist" arguments became more trenchant. His extensive reading about beliefs and practices of North American indigenous peoples gave him many examples of non-hierarchical, non-sexist ways of organizing society. He cited them often in discussions.

Sixteen

The Unattached Intellectual in Detroit

The printing co-op was among the most successful and tangible of Fredy's Detroit projects. Even though fewer and fewer people used its resources, Fredy was pleased that he himself could print what he wrote; he also liked having access to camera and darkroom. After 1975, maintaining the print shop took little time. By then, Black & Red was able to pay most of the expenses; *Radical America* was printed on the east coast. Occasionally, with help from friends, we did a "commercial" job for Marty Glaberman or for anarchist comrades in Toronto. But by 1979, the increasing deterioration of the building which housed the co-op made it clear that it was impossible to keep it functioning at the Michigan Avenue location. Makeshift arrangements to protect the equipment and paper from the leaking roof were inadequate. Fredy's commitment to maintain the print shop did not extend to a commitment to move and re-install it. In 1970, when the space had been transformed from an auto collision shop into a work space for printing, there had been dozens of enthusiastic collaborators, most of them impatient to put the new facility to use. By the end of the decade, Fredy saw that few people in Detroit felt a need for printing equipment that they could operate personally. Building another print shop was not a project Fredy cared to undertake on his own. "Besides," he said, "I spent a decade on this project. It was rewarding but a ten-year commitment is long enough."

Disposing of the printing equipment was discouraging. Once Fredy had ascertained that there were few eager recipients, he left the bulk of the task to others. In March 1980 an anarchist collective from Ann Arbor took most of the machinery and fittings. Their moving expenses were paid by the sale of outdated, unused film which remained from the 1971 auction purchase. (In 1980, silver prices had skyrocketed and Millard Berry found a buyer willing to pay $1500 for the film.)

Conversations with some of the people from the Ann Arbor collective did not make us hopeful about the success of their undertaking. Although the equipment was acquired and moved without cost to them, they would soon be obliged to spend large sums for a place to house it. Some in the group had the rudiments of printing skills, but they weren't prepared—even had they wanted to—to use the equipment for commercial work. We didn't think they had found a reasonable solution to the financial problem. Even less auspicious was their admission that they didn't have anything they really wanted to print. Knowing how much effort it took to install the machines and adjust them to working order, we feared they might sit unused until they were sold for junk. This is possibly what actually happened.

Fredy accepted with equanimity the end of the printing co-op but he was not ready to drop the Black & Red project. In the last months of the co-op, we reprinted several of the publications so that when all the boxes were moved to the basement of our house on Porter Street, we had a good supply of most of the titles on our list. (B & R books published after 1980 were printed in a commercial shop; we continued to do typesetting and layout ourselves.)

Fredy never had aspirations for Black & Red to become a large publishing house. The goal of the initial project was to promote communication between individuals; to a large extent, the goal was reached. A reader's response often led to an exchange of correspondence and this, in Fredy's eyes, proved the project's success. An urge to craftsmanship also motivated the Black & Red project. Fredy had high standards for the publications' appearance and he enjoyed both the creative and the meticulous aspects of designing a book; typos distressed him. Commercial success was never a goal: prices asked for the publications covered only the cost of producing them, plus a small margin which allowed us to send free copies to friends and those unable to pay for them. Fredy considered it appropriate that the author be responsible for tasks associated with correspondence and packaging, and he did them willingly.

The press run of publications was always small. Except for three titles, the number of copies distributed hasn't exceeded 5,000. Fredy was satisfied with the scale of the publishing project, but that is not to say he was content with the number of readers his books reached. Once he put them out in the world (explicitly without a copyright), he hoped others would print and distribute additional copies. A number of Fredy's writings did, in fact, appear (in English and translation) in Argentina, North America and Europe through the efforts of appreciative readers.

The projects undertaken by Detroit friends depended, like the Black & Red project, on human energy, not capital. Their implicit, and sometimes explicit, message was: you, too, can do what we're doing. Fredy observed that he never had heard of a single project proposed by North American leftists that had foundered solely for lack of money. Fredy took genuine pleasure in following his friends' progress as they realized a project.

Terri and Kemal Orcan and Ahmet Zeren rehabilitated a burned out storefront in our neighborhood and made of it an exceptionally congenial restaurant which served superlative Turkish food. Occasional poetry readings took place at this Bagley Cafe and it was here that a memorial gathering for Fredy was held in August 1985.

Detroit friends involved in media projects were, like Fredy, wary of a project outgrowing manageable, human bounds. Though great care was taken to equal the readability and attractiveness of their commercial counterparts, "mass" media was a realm to shun, an area permeated by hierarchy and one-way communication.

Ralph Franklin's broadside, *The Daily Barbarian*, ran little risk of co-optation or bureaucratic takeover since, its name notwithstanding, the number of publications averaged fewer than one per year.

The *Fifth Estate*, founded in 1965, had a more ample and variegated history, but after 1975 it was unequivocally a non-commercial, anti-hierarchical project. Letters from readers continue to be an important part of the paper, and articles expressing diverse perspectives appear in its pages.

In January 1981, Ralph and Alan Franklin along with two friends inaugurated a rock band, the Layabouts, from its origins a non-commercial venture. They performed mostly songs written by members in the band. The players subsidized the project themselves. In 1985, the group announced that any proceeds from their forthcoming record would be used to further community activities.

Except to help out with typesetting the *Fifth Estate,* Fredy did not participate in his friends' projects. Once the print shop closed in 1980, he did not engage in collective projects which could be considered "political." The expectation that tomorrow everything could change (which followed the 1968 events in Paris) had dissipated by the early 1980s. I think Fredy still believed what he wrote in the inaugural issue of *Black & Red,* that "Anything Can Happen," but his vision of a better society did not provide him with a program for collaboration with others.

In his 1983 letter to Piri, the Hungarian emigré living in London,* Fredy referred to himself as an "almost total recluse." As a "recluse," Fredy worked alone, with intensity, on his self-defined projects, but his life was anything but solitary. A day without visitors was the exception, not the rule. In addition to shared meals with friends and frequent musical sessions, intellectual exchanges were common. With Jeff Gilbert he discussed the languages, cultural traits and histories of North American indigenous peoples. Jeff's extensive knowledge of geography and the histories of people on other continents as well, made him a receptive and critical listener to Fredy's early formulations of themes which appear in *Against His-story, Against Leviathan!*

Kemal Orcan's revulsion to bureaucracy and antagonism to mercenary motives led him to study earlier social modes in order to find precedents for his own choices. Consuming numerous cups of coffee and cigarettes, he and Fredy had wide-ranging discussions about mythologies, Islam, communities where non-conformists enhanced the lives of all, possible ways to escape the money nexus. They both liked the books of Mircea Eliade. The variety of world-views found in Eliade's studies on world religions stimulated them to analyze their own tenets and those held by their contemporaries.

Subjects of more local concern usually predominated when Fredy was with *Fifth Estate* friends. Proud of their public actions, this group readily accepted the title, "Eat the Rich Gang." Their jocular reports kept Fredy informed about the leftist milieu in Detroit and around the country. Applying Jacques Camatte's insight that the needs of Capital are commonly articulated by a political avant-garde, the articles in their quarterly newspaper made profound and scathing critiques of programs and slogans advocated by "progressive" gangs. David Watson signed many of his *Fifth Estate* articles "Mr. Venom."

Fredy's observation that "ideas are in the air" was borne out again in the late 1970s: the Eat the Rich Gang, like Fredy, took up a

*See page 94.

primitivist perspective in order to evaluate the society we live in. Concern for Mother Earth and the antagonism to technology and its demands, made Western-oriented economic and political history seem narrow in scope. "Mr. Venom" began signing some of his articles "Primitivo Solis."

Impelled by events in the world outside, Fredy frequently emerged from his "reclusiveness." He attended most local demonstrations against U.S. intervention in Central America. When the U.S. Marines invaded Grenada in 1983, he joined many others walking up and down in front of the Federal Building in downtown Detroit. He was repelled by most of the slogans shouted by demonstrators, slogans like "Yankee, no! Cuba, si!"

Hostile to all slogans, Fredy chose the printed word to respond to certain current events. The willingness of the *Fifth Estate* staff to print his essays encouraged Fredy to interrupt his long-range projects to write them.

The September 1977 *Fifth Estate* carried "Ten Theses on the Proliferation of Egocrats" written by Fredy.* This is an abbreviated version of an argument in Velli's *Manual,* here used to criticize the commercial and missionary practices of specifically anarchist and libertarian militants. A *Fifth Estate* reader had objected to the newspaper's attacks on the Montreal-based Black Rose Books: "When 'libertarians' slanderously trash others, I question their maturity and commitment to revolutionary change." In Thesis IV, Fredy quotes this objection and then scornfully criticizes the militant who defends his commercial ventures by insisting that in order to propagate his message he is "concentrating heavily on distribution and promotion." Fredy contends that "[t]he anti-totalitarian revolution requires, not another medium, but the liquidation of all media."

In 1979, following the radioactive leak from the nuclear reactor at Three Mile Island in Pennsylvania, Fredy wrote "Progress and Nuclear Power." He pointed out that this poisoning of the living inhabitants was only the most recent in a series that began "eleven score years ago" and insisted that this event was no "accident":

> — The poisoning of people in Eastern Pennsylvania with cancer-inducing radiation by a system that devotes a substantial portion of its activity to "defense" against nuclear assault from abroad,

*In this issue of the *Fifth Estate* there was also a review of Gary Snyder's *The Old Ways,* a now-classic statement of a primitivist perspective.

—The contamination of food which is to be consumed by
the continent's remaining inhabitants, and the destruction of the
prospects of farmers who had dutifully devoted their lives to
growing the merchandise interesting to Capital at a stage which
ended half a century ago,
    —The transformation into a literal minefield, using un-
precedentedly lethal poisons and explosives, of a continent once
peopled by human beings whose aim in life was to enjoy the
air, sun, trees, animals and each other,
    —The prospect of a continent covered with raging infer-
nos, their loudspeakers reciting their recorded messages to a
charred earth: "There is no need to overreact; the situation is
stable; the leaders have everything under control,"
    —all this is no accident. It is the present stage of progress
of Technology, alias Capital, called Frankenstein by Mary
Wollstonecraft Shelley, considered "neutral" by aspiring
managers burning to get their "revolutionary" hands on the con-
trols. For two hundred years Capital developed by destroying
nature, by removing and destroying human beings. Capital has
now begun a frontal attack on its own domestics; its computers
have begun to calculate the expendability of those who'd been
taught to think themselves its beneficiaries.*

"Anti-Semitism and the Beirut Pogrom" appeared in the Winter
1982 *Fifth Estate*. Fredy wrote it the previous summer, shortly before
the connivance of the Israeli army permitted the massacres in the
Sabra-Shatilla refugee camps. Using his own history and youthful
perceptions as a context for his changing views about Zionism, Fredy's
essay concludes by denouncing the know-nothing "American" qualities
that make many Jewish-Americans cheerleaders for Israel.
    Shortly after the Israeli army's 1967 *Blitzkrieg*, Fredy did have
a heated argument with his "Americanized" aunt (the one who serves
as prototype for the position he attacks), but the direct motivation
(in July 1982) of this essay was a comment, over dinner, by an
acquaintance—more American than Jewish—about the Arabs: "But
they're so *dirty!*" Fredy felt that his angry rejoinder at the dinner table
was an inadequate response to the "bad faith" exhibited by the woman's
self-righteous racist assertion. Fredy's differences with her were not
over "facts"; he asked himself how the two of them had come to
opposite points of view. "Anti-Semitism and the Beirut Pogrom" grew

*"Progress and Nuclear Power" appeared in the issue of the *Fifth Estate* dated April
18, 1979.

out of his probing the assumptions which allow past persecution to justify subsequent racist practices toward others.

In the essay Fredy does not attribute his insights about the transformation of victims into victimizers to his narrow escape from a concentration camp. Neither his childhood in a land of Quechuas nor his coming of age in the land of the heroic pioneer led him to question the guidelines for success in "America." He writes that it was things he learned "from books equally accessible to others" and his "starting to empathize with victims of oppression" that led him to look critically at the Zionist pioneer endeavor.

Indignation over a leftist author's political program led Fredy to write "The Continuing Appeal of Nationalism" which appeared in the December 1984 *Fifth Estate*. Looking at specific national liberation struggles in the U.S., Russia, Israel and Germany, Fredy concludes:

> The liberation of the nation is the last stage in the elimination of parasites. Capitalism had already earlier cleared nature of parasites and reduced most of the rest of nature to raw materials for processing industries. Modern national socialism or social nationalism holds out the prospect of eliminating parasites from human society as well...Hitler's (and the Zionists') treatment of the nation as a racial entity was another central tenet [of modern liberation Thought]. The cadres were recruited from among people depleted of their ancestors' kinships and customs, and consequently the liberators were not distinguishable from the oppressors in terms of language, beliefs, customs or weapons; the only welding material that held them to each other and to their mass base was the welding material that had held white servants to white bosses on the American frontier; the "racial bond" gave identities to those without identity, kinship to those who had no kin, community to those who had lost their community; it was the last bond of the culturally depleted. [pp. 48, 51 in the Black & Red edition]

When publishing this essay as a Black & Red pamphlet in January 1985, Fredy included black and white reproductions of collages from Velli's *Manual*. The graphics link this essay with the 1972 satire of leadership and serve as a reproachful reminder that Velli's message had not been widely communicated or understood. When undertaking the exposure of revolutionary leaders thirteen years earlier, a critique of nationalism had seemed superfluous.

In February and March 1985, Fredy interrupted work on *The Strait* to write two essays reclaiming Hawthorne as a fellow critic, not a celebrator, of the Invaders' takeover of this continent. For several years Fredy had been studying the many resisters to the progress imposed by the arrogant Europeans, and he recognized that Melville, Hawthorne and Thoreau had helped him enormously to distinguish the fraudulent from the authentic. "To the New York Review of B" and "On the Machine in the Garden" were printed in the *Fifth Estate* after Fredy's death. They appeared in the October 1985 issue, on pages following the announcement of Fredy's death on July 26th and David Watson's "Appreciation" of their comrade. Fredy had himself typeset his articles several weeks before he died.

His introduction to the essays reads:

> Critiques of economic development, material progress, technology and industry are not a discovery of the *Fifth Estate*. Human beings resisted the incursions from the earliest days, and many of North America's best-known 19th century writers, among them Melville, Hawthorne and Thoreau, were profound critics of the technological society. Since these writers became "classics of American literature," and therefore available to all interested readers, defenders of official views have had to carry on a "cold war" against them. The most powerful weapon has been the classroom assignment; most students attacked by this weapon never again cracked a book by a "classic." Other ways of "conquering and pacifying" the classics have been more subtle: the authors were maligned, the works were misinterpreted, the critiques were diverted and at times inverted.
>
> The two essays below are descriptions of some of the methods used in this "cold war." The first was submitted to (but not published in) the official organ of the "cold warriors," *The New York Review of B*. The second, originally a letter, attempts to unravel and expose the diversions and inversions of one of the more influential "cold warriors."

Fredy's initial anger came from the insidious credence which a reviewer in a national journal gave to the undocumented accusation that Hawthorne had had incestuous relations with his sister; accompanying the review article was a caricature of Hawthorne, a large I emblazoned on his chest. Fredy understood that those who chafed under Hawthorne's denunciation of bigotry would always welcome an opportunity to discredit the denouncer; he wrote these essays not to defend Hawthorne from an unsubstantiated accusation but to express his outrage at authoritative interpreters of Hawthorne's work who twist his meaning. Leo Marx, the reviewer in question, had earlier introduced and appended another Hawthorne story to a popular edition of *The Scarlet Letter*. Fredy argues that in doing this, Marx was attempting to distort the author's message to make it seem to say the opposite.

Fredy musters considerable ironic eloquence and logical wit to denounce this falsification. He concludes his essay "To the New York Review of B" by insisting that if the opening scene of *The Scarlet Letter* were shifted to the 1980s, Leo Marx as well as the incest accuser would certainly be among the bigots standing on the platform provided by *The New York Review of Bigotry,* all of them looking down on the sinner Hester displaying the A on her breast.

An earlier interruption of work on *The Strait* resulted in an essay of 300 pages, *Against His-story, Against Leviathan!* The first two chapters appeared in the Winter 1982-83 *Fifth Estate* before Fredy had completed the entire work.

By the fall of 1982, Fredy had already devoted six years to a study of the European Invader's appropriation of the North American continent; reading Frederick Turner's *Beyond Geography* he was startled by the similarity of Turner's conclusions to his own and reminded of how long the "Western Spirit Against the Wilderness" (the subtitle of Turner's book) had been domesticating living creatures. "Leviathan" was the label Fredy gave to the machine-like beast which, in the guise of divine authority, the state or commerce, posed as humanity's friend but which, in fact, devoured all natural organisms. Fredy called Leviathan's own account of its trajectory "His-story."

Asserting that "resistance is the only human component of the entire His-story," Fredy suspended his in-depth study of resistance to Leviathanic incursions in the woodlands around the Great Lakes to examine the "barbarians" and untamed tribes who, in earlier times, unequivocally refused the bondage of civilization. Where His-story exults in civic and military achievements, calling them Progress, Fredy's story views each consolidation of state power as an encroachment on the human community. He addresses the reader as one individual speaking to another and makes no claim to follow scholarly rules: "I take it for granted that resistance is the natural human response to dehumanization and, therefore, does not have to be explained or justified" (page 184). The resistance story follows the chronology of Leviathan's destructive march, but avoids using His-storians' conventions of dating the events. This, as well as the poetic visionary language, gives the work an epic quality.

Fredy compiled the events of his story largely from Leviathanic His-storians. Using the works of one of them, Norman Cohn, as an example, Fredy explains how he was able to discover the resister's anger in spite of the His-storian's defamatory words.

> A man called Norman Cohn, a friend of authority, law and order, will in our time document a millennium of resistance, maligning every episode of it.
>
> A serious scholar is one who takes the Pope at his word and discounts the words of rebels. A ranter is one who takes the rebels at their word and discounts every word of the Pope. Cohn will be a solid, serious scholar, not a fanatical, ranting extremist. The words of authorities, especially the police, will be his rock, his positive evidence.
>   . . .
> Cohn's peers, professors who will massacre Vietnamese peasants from desks at a State University will pretend to be appalled by atrocities of Calleys who turn the professors' words into deeds, but the professors' real rage will be against the resisters who turn their weapons against the Calleys. The serious professors will heap all the deflected violence, Authority's own violence, on the heads of the rebels resisting Authority's violence.
>   . . .
> Many of the resisters are convinced that by their own efforts they can evade the transformations . . . which in their eyes can only immiserate and maim human beings. . .
>
> An individual intimately familiar with the daily rapacity may remain unmoved by critics of the rapacity. She or he must make a choice, she must decide to turn against the authorities and to join the circle of resisters. Such a decision disrupts a person's whole life, and it needs to be motivated by very good reasons. The good reasons are expressed in the language of the time, not in the language of some future time. A revelation or a visitation is a very good reason. The revelation might come in a dream, or in a vision, or in what we will call a complete mental breakdown. Before this experience, everything was noise and nothing had meaning. After the experience, everything is clear. Now the individual wonders why others are so blind. She might

become impatient with the others and leave them to their blindness, or she might decide to return to the others to help them see.

All this is very understandable, very human, and it has been
taking place in human communities for a long time. But such
sudden disruptions of individual lives are also disruptions of
Leviathanic existence. After such experiences, an individual
abandons the sequence of meaningless intervals of Leviathanic
Time and recovers some of the rhythms of communities in the
state of nature.

This is why Leviathanic His-storians will discount, malign
and try to exorcise such experiences. Contempt and ridicule will
be favorite weapons of the serious scholars who will pretend
to give unbiased accounts.

Norman Cohn, for example, will go out of his way to talk
about the revelations of the millennarian resisters. He needs say
no more. Equally armored readers will immediately share
Cohn's contempt toward individuals who are so pathological as
to be guided by their own dreams and visions. The scholar and
his armored readers will take it for granted that only the revelations of judges and scholars have validity.

Cohn's ridicule will reach heights of scholarly contempt
when he tells of individuals who consider themselves Messiahs,
who convince themselves that their efforts can help to save
Mankind from Leviathanic dehumanization, enslavement and
doom. Cohn need not exclaim: How naive! How criminal! How
well deserved the jailing, the torture, the hanging, the burning!
Such exclamations will come automatically to readers who consider duly constituted authorities the only possible saviors of
mankind and Leviathan the only possible Messiah. [pp. 183-188]

Academic apologists for the status quo were not alone in earning
Fredy's vitriolic scorn in *Against His-story*. The European-born
pioneers, carriers of Puritan virtues to this continent, are no longer
characterized as sturdy yeomen as they had been in *The New Freedom:
Corporate Capitalism*. Armed with destructive technology and
"armored" with a nature-hating ideology, these bringers of destruction to the woodlands and lakes around Detroit were themselves
victims of Leviathanic domination. In *The Strait* Fredy let some of
the characters indigenous to this continent discover the Europeans'
prior subjugation — in this way attributing to these individuals an almost
superhuman understanding and generosity unlikely to co-exist with
their tragic experiences. In *Against His-story* Fredy was more severe.

Here, his harsh judgment of the pioneers comes at the end of the
long and rich story of resistance to kings and priests. He uses Sartrean
psychology to assert that these trail-blazers for Civilization, these
zeks determined to universalize their own condition by blindly
invading Eden, *did* have other choices.

> The last Leviathan's zeks are not conscripts but volunteers.
> . . . Tasks imposed by force on earlier zeks are taken up as
> Callings by the volunteers. . . The volunteer zek does not resent
> the sellers who ruined him, for he is himself one of them. . . He
> resents. . . those whom he calls Renegades, namely fellow zeks
> who make themselves at home in communities of the continent's
> survivors. His bitterest passion is reserved for the decimated
> communities in which the Renegades find refuge. The beings
> in those communities are not human to him. . . [T]he good-for-
> nothings, the Cannibals, pretend that food simply offers itself
> to them on its own, they hunt and fish like Nabobs or ancient
> noblemen, they spend their days as well as their nights howling
> and jumping like demented wolves.
>   Were the pioneer to admit their humanity, however brief-
> ly, however grudgingly, his innards would explode, his armor
> melt, his mask fall, for he would in that flash of light see himself
> as a zek, his freedom as self-enslavement, his market-
> Civilization as a forced-labor camp. The devil would try to tempt
> him to become a Renegade and, irony of ironies, he would fall,
> unlike Eve, out of blessed labor into cursed Eden. [pp. 267-9]

Work on *Against His-story,* itself an interruption of work on *The
Strait,* was suspended in November 1982 while we moved from the
Porter Street row house to a house on Vinewood, in the same
southwest Detroit neighborhood. Falling prices of property in the
city made it possible for us to buy — on "time" — the large house with
a pleasant back yard. Before moving in we made extensive internal
renovations, getting rid of the dropped ceilings, the fluorescent lights
and black paneling. We paid some professionals to help us, but
numerous friends donated their skills. Peter Werbe wielded a wrecking
bar as if the black paneling were a destroyer of community; and Terri
and Kemal Orcan handled hammer, yardstick and paintbrush as if
a growing fellowship depended on their dexterous use.

After arranging his workspace, installing the cello, assembling
garden seeds and tools, and organizing the books (at which time
Lenin's *Collected Works* were banished to an attic shelf which also

held Samuelson's *Principles of Economics*), Fredy resumed his daily routine. The refurbished premises did not turn out to be a home for a new community, but Fredy and I did share them with many friends. One of the first large gatherings we hosted in the Vinewood house was in honor of the publication of *Against His-story, Against Leviathan!* Several dozen friends joined us in June 1983 to celebrate the event.

Seventeen

The Strait

In 1977, Fredy gave a preliminary title to the historical study of the world-changers he had undertaken: "The Rise and Fall of Capital and Labor." The focus was to be on Capital, personified by Sabellicus, and on its dialectical inversion, personified by Sabina, Capital's daughter, the mirror of production.* In the ensuing years, Fredy abandoned much of his original conception, perhaps seeing it as another version of His-story. But he was still determined to write his exposé of the world-changers. This was the work he had been preparing to write since he left Columbia University in 1959. He aspired to incorporate in a unified account the many things he knew about the nefarious effects of commodities and technology; about the inadequacies of all institutions; the numerous ways of being a toady; the hazards of one speaking to many and, of course, about saviors who claim to protect their followers from all of the above.

To avoid His-story's clutches, Fredy turned to a non-linear interpretation of human events. This new approach tremendously expanded the setting of the story. Becoming acquainted with non-Leviathanic views of the world, he came to see as narrow arrogance the study of exclusively human interactions. In his new guides' interpretations of the world, all living beings were included.

With humility, Fredy tried to absorb the teachings of the North American shamen and "rememberers" whose insights often originated in an era preceding the arrival of Europeans. He read the powerful denunciations and appeals of people who disliked the world-changers'

*Four pages of Fredy's early notes are reproduced in the Appendix.

ways and whose heritage provided a perspective for rejecting them. He also read memoirs of individuals, legends of a people, and about the significance of rituals. Always a lover of words, Fredy was entranced by the eloquence of these texts and convinced by the writers' visions. He read scholarly treatises as well; though he was often angered by their reductive condescension, they led him to original sources.

In his notes Fredy wrote messages to himself about the crucial importance of the story being "oral." His goal was to emerge with a song. He was surely aware that the hundreds of characters would not make the story easy to read, nor would the avoidance of the Invaders' system of dates make the chronology obvious. But this story, emulating its oral predecessors, could not have recourse to the European establishment's dating system.* Births, deaths, plagues and battles correlate events described by Obenabi and Wabnokwe, the narrators of Fredy's story. As setting, he chose the place in which he was living; the title of the work is the English translation of "Detroit."

The epic Fredy created *needed* all the individual characters. From his own experience Fredy knew that resistance to domination takes many forms. The choices made by a free people, individuals neither domesticated nor fettered by the dominators' own ideology, fascinated him. He tried to put himself in their situation, hoping that their responses might help in his own efforts to resist. From fragments, he rounded out a personality and created a world of richly diverse women and men. Although some characters are taken as archetypes of their milieu, they never are mere representatives. Before choosing names, Fredy made for each "people" a list of names he had found while reading about their past. When a dictionary of words was available (as in *History of the Ottawa and Chippewa Indians of Michigan* by A.J. Blackbird), he constructed original names. Many characters have European names in addition to the descriptive appellation given them by kin. Although never mentioned explicitly in the finished story, Obenabi also answers to Benjamin J. Burr-net, Wabnokwe to Rebekah Burr-net. Some historical characters who spend long periods among Rootkin have non-European names. Thus John Con-err is known to Obenabi exclusively as Bijiki. The Labadie family figures prominently in events on the Strait and in Mishilimakina; Baptiste, Antoine (Le Sauteur) and Paulette appear as Batì, Lesotér and Pamoko, respectively.

*In fact, Fredy usually shunned the use of annual chronology. In only one of his published works did he incorporate dates into the text.

The reader of the first volume of *The Strait,* "Book of Obenabi,
His Songs," finds self-possessed characters who know who they are
and who attempt to live harmoniously in their social and natural
environment. A coherent sense of self is essential to their well-being.
The reader may regard the expropriation of their lands and the diminu-
tion of their possibilities as tragic, but few of the people Obenabi
tells about view themselves as victims of a malign fate. When there
is personal tragedy it usually results from an individual's disorientation, a failure to know who one is. Although Fredy treated the traditional use of the dream lodges in an ironic way (most dreams allow
for contradictory interpretations), self-understanding, situating oneself
in the world, is an aspiration Fredy took very seriously.

Obenabi's "Songs" open with a dream sequence that recapitulates
his and his ancestors' lives. In the course of the dream Obenabi
traverses the lives of his ancestors in a floating fashion, hurtling
backward in time; continental migrations are covered in a few
sentences. Obenabi's view of who he is begins with the emergence
of life on the planet. This "journey to the beginning" confuses the
reader just as his own dreams confuse Obenabi. As the "songs" resume
chronological time, the dream's *personae,* Obenabi's grandmothers,
become known; their actions, significant. Obenabi explains that the
dreams preceded his understanding, sometimes by long periods of
time.

A gestation period of nine months preceded Obenabi's dream
birth. The first six trace the story of human existence from the
emergence of life from water to the 1640s and are undifferentiated
(at least to me). As Yahatase, the first grandmother whose name
Obenabi knows, receives the mask from her predecessor, she observes
that six moonless nights have passed since her journey began. The
mask is subsequently worn by Miogwewe and Katabwe before the
"I" of the narrator is Obenabi himself.

As a conscious incarnation of his grandmothers, Obenabi sings
of their lives. He tells of the choices made by those who are much
but have little when confronted by those who have much but are little.
Some, like his ancient grandmother Yahatase, strive to isolate her
people from the Invaders and want the latter driven into the salt sea.
Her companion, Wedasi, is a conciliator, keen to avoid bloodshed.
With proseletyzing zeal Yahatase's daughter Shutaha endeavors to
convert the newcomers to Rootkin ways. Ubankiko is enamored of
the Invaders' objects which she shamelessly pursues. Menoko detests
conflict and refuses to acknowledge the possibility of a non-nurturing

world. Adaptable Mota learns how to "trade." Although suspicious, Chacapwe accepts as neighbors on the Strait a small number of the unusual newcomers. Generations before Obenabi's birth, westward-bound emigrés from the eastern seaboard warn woodland Rootkin that only by retreating to a land without Invaders, to a place far from trade and commerce, can they preserve their ancestors' ways.

Obenabi recognizes that these very different responses come from individuals who know who they are. He sees his contemporaries making comparable choices. Obenabi generally respects his kin's responses; he knows they have reasons for what they do. As distasteful as commerce is to Obenabi, he acknowledges that his mother's adoption of the trader Burr-net and the existence of Bison Prairie as a fur-trading center provides a material basis for maintaining Rootkin and some semblance of their ways. One of the few times Obenabi judges his kin negatively is when he objects to his cousin Shabeni's efforts to mobilize all Rootkin into a unified army to drive the Invader away.

> Shabeni's answer angered me. I had never before had a standpoint from which I could think of someone as a traitor. Shabeni had built my dream lodges; he had been my cousin, guide and companion. But I knew that his single people with a single army had not been born on the ashes of Kithepekanu, but had been carried across the Ocean on the ships that brought firewater, rifles and plagues. [p. 360]

Madness was the lot of two of Obenabi's grandmothers: Yahatase and Menoko. Rebellious Yahatase because she was helpless to protect her kin from the devastation she and her sister had known as children; gentle Menoko because the incomprehensible and painful experiences she endured should have been impossible in a world which, in her conception, was wondrous and good. Their madness in no way indicates that they lacked a coherent view of themselves.

Alcoholism and suicide are choices made by some of Obenabi's contemporaries, specifically his brother Nashkowatak and his nephew Wimego. Obenabi understands that his close kin turn to these solutions because they do not know who they are. Another brother, Chebansi, is equally disoriented; after definitively fleeing from the Invaders' society on the Strait, Chebansi ironically spends the rest of his life in Bison Prairie carrying on the fur-trade. The incapacitating dread he experienced as a youth causes Chebansi to conduct all dealings with the Invaders through intermediaries. His fear never leaves him.

Obenabi, like his brothers and most of his kin, fears the Invaders. Living in the early nineteenth century, he has little hope that he will be able either to turn them back beyond the salt sea or that he and his people can adopt them. For a time, he considers leaving the Peninsula to seek a distant land that will be free of Invaders, but his dream on the Strait's shore turns him from that path.

Obenabi does not understand the Invaders, but he does understand himself. In the idyllic weeks spent with Udatonte, Obenabi was in harmony with the world; he experienced the joy of life. To help in his quest to recover this joy, he counts among his strengths the knowledge willed to him by generations of kin, the properties of renewal furnished by the woodlands and waters of his home and the certainty that ecstasy exists.

I learned from notes for *The Strait* that in the twentieth century Obenabi's material link with his ancestors, his cherished bundle, is destroyed. His *Songs* survive, however, and link us to him and to them. The strengths Obenabi could count on, fragile enough in his day, seem even less substantial in this epoch of further encroachment by the Invader. Fredy's "remembering" efforts invite us to nurture them.

If Fredy's acquaintance with Obenabi's world came more from books than from experience, he was altogether familiar with the world of Wabnokwe, Obenabi's sister. Her "Tales," Book Two of *The Strait* ("preserved," like Book One, by nephew Robert Dupré) are what remain of Fredy's Sabellicus-Sabina story, the world of Capital and resistance to Capital. Here one finds business, culture, mobilization of armies, struggles for political hegemony. Among the participants are nationalists, educators, fund-raisers and pacifists. Musicians and intellectuals too. Fredy, like Wabnokwe, claimed music and intellectual pursuits as part of the movement to resist Capital. Both came to recognize that the claim was dubious.

The mission Wabnokwe sets for herself is to synthesize her Potawatomie heritage with the traditions of the French Enlightenment. But the world of Capital devours her undertaking: Wabnokwe is cheated of her property by a cultured old-world revolutionary; greedy landsuckers, when they don't resort to violence, use cheating treaties to gain their ends; sexual repression takes a large toll among Wabnokwe's friends.

Her story records some of the fraudulent techniques which transform Tiosa Rondion (the Iroquois name for the village on the Strait's shore) into a bustling commercial center; it also tells of the increasing domestication of the inhabitants. Four short generations after Chacapwe allows some Invaders to lodge near her village, the Strait's residents are unable to prevent Belle Isle from becoming the possession of a newly-arrived Invader; they turn to "civil" authorities to register their protest.

Details from Detroit's history—the fires, the background of influential families, the expropriations, the political intrigues—are carefully researched, as is the geographic setting. Fredy prepared a map locating, among other sites, the Labadie house, the springhill burial ground and the schoolhouse which later was used as a grain depot.

Fredy intentionally left inexplicit many details about his characters but he provided abundant clues to permit the discovery of additional features. For example, an attentive reader should be able to determine which languages are spoken: Wabnokwe and Obenabi converse in Potawatomie; in the opening pages of Book One Obenabi comments on Wabnokwe's French accent when she greets him. Non-business conversations in the Jay-may household are in French. Misus Bay-con's school is conducted in English; the fact that the majority of pupils do not understand it gives Gabinya the opportunity to insert himself and successfully abduct Greta-may. Obenabi transmits his "songs" to his nephew in the Potawatomie tongue. Wabnokwe writes her journals in French. Fredy's pleasure in his own ability to converse in four languages disposed him to set his story in a milieu where people spoke in several tongues.

One character in *The Strait* who is fluent in at least four languages is Robert Dupré, nephew of the narrators. Fredy expects the reader to remember that Dupré is the great-great-grandson of the cultured Haitian who founded Chicago and that Obenabi's father is the trader Burr-net. Thus, in his notes for the brief interlude passages whose setting is the Detroit jail in 1851, Fredy wrote that the jailers—with the eyes of racist Americans—see uncle and nephew, "the two prisoners leaning against the jailhouse wall, as an old white man whispering to a somewhat younger black man."*

*Fredy's original plan for presenting the two-volume work was to pose as translator of a text written by Robert Dupré. The unpublished manuscript, in French, was to have been discovered among the belongings of one of Dupré's descendants, Ted Nasibu. Since Fredy's formulation of this deception was far from complete, I was unable to carry it out.

The conscious resisters to Capital are central to the second volume of *The Strait*. Fredy's familiarity with this world permitted him to analyze the resistance in detail and to draw characters with complex personalities. He evaluates his characters' choices but, never underestimating the difficulties of finding an effective and radical path, he does not judge them harshly. Counting himself among the dissidents he wrote about, Fredy sympathetically records their abilities as well as their frailties.

The school established by Wabnokwe and three friends is an institution which serves to domesticate Rootkin youth. Dehcnyante, an intellectual well-acquainted with European radical traditions, recognizes its function from the start. But in Beth's view, the school serves as a bulwark against the Invader since it permits her, as teacher, to transmit Rootkin history and traditions to her disoriented kin. Wabnokwe rejoices in the prospect of the school linking the Rootkin heritage with the principles of the French Revolution. In fact, Wabnokwe sees herself as ideally suited to carry out a synthesis of the best in two ways of life. For her, the Strait is not only where she chooses to live. It symbolizes the proximity of two cultures; she yearns to serve as a bridge between them. Her enthusiasm blinds her to political and military realities which, in the early 1800s, were leading her kin to ally with the British. Wabnokwe's contempt for the soldiers and supporters of the British monarchy leads her to further the cause of their adversary, the bluecoated Americans. Certain that she is supporting the progressive side, she uses her feminine charms and her rhetorical abilities to encourage the defeat of the Redcoats and their allies. In Wabnokwe's view, the British are the biggest threat to her goal of bridging two cultures. She refuses to credit reports about the desolation wrought by deceitful and cruel bluecoated armies.

Fredy did not consider an absurd delusion the goal sought by Wabnokwe, Chacapwe and Shutaha to integrate the Potawatomie and French cultures. Before the dominance of the Anglo-Saxons, Detroit was culturally and racially mixed. It was during Wabnokwe's lifetime that the imported racism became an unassailable foundation of the society. At Wabnokwe's funeral in 1841, her nephew Robert Dupré hears the remark of an onlooker: "She was very intelligent, for a halfbreed." Thus, on the very terrain where she and her Rootkin ancestors had lived and were buried, an area now trampled by the Invader, a racial slur presumes to obliterate Wabnokwe's cultural achievements and her generous aspirations.

Wabnokwe's mood in the 1830s contrasts sharply with her former confidence and certainty about her chosen course of action. The early chapters of Book Two give expression to Wabnokwe's exhilaration at being a world-changer, and her joy at having a central place in Le Monde, a social group in its ascendancy. Certain that she knows what needs to be done and confident that she and her likes can realize their goals, she scorns the Killer Brookses and considers quaint her brother Obenabi's attachment to the bundle of ancestral objects given to him by their grandmother Katabwe.

At a moment of crisis, however, Wabnokwe's self-image as a bridge between two cultures assumes horrifying implications for her. In a passage in her journal Wabnokwe asks if aspirations similar to hers had motivated others who, in earlier periods, had wanted to bridge two cultures. If so, their efforts brought desolation to their kin. With a view to dispelling illusions she examines all the similarities between herself and five female predecessors: Dante's Beatriche, Malinche, Pocahantas, Angelík Kuyeryé and her own mother Cakima. Wabnokwe's painful conclusion is that she has lived up to the name her mother had given her: Dawn, Easterner. "She [had] succeeded in becoming a sun that burned the people, animals and trees of Kichigami."

By the end of Book Two of *The Strait* it is clear that Wabnokwe is no longer a sun. The attentive reader can observe that her actual social role is that of a household domestic. Although the house in which she lives and works, as well as the power wielded by its owner, came from the furs her parents and her uncle had provided to Jay-may, Wabnokwe's access to the house is solely through the back door. The days when she was the shining light of the musical and intellectual salon are over. Since then, Wabnokwe's social status has been in decline: from poor relative and governess she becomes a mere servant.

Dehenyante, the radical intellectual, who after the war of 1812 becomes Wabnokwe's companion, shares Wabnokwe's enthusiasm for the French Revolution, but he sees much sooner than she that its goals have been betrayed. Dehenyante (whose name means Rainbow) is a partisan of neither side in the 1812 war. He chooses to fight the Invader's way of life rather than Invader armies; he leaves the Strait to assist in the resistance to factory work in east coast cities. He returns to his family for occasional visits; when his daughters are older, they too leave Wabnokwe and the Strait to become Abolitionists and labor activists.

The workers in the eastern city are betrayed by their leaders who make peace with Tammany Hall. Dehenyante writes to Wabnokwe about his disappointment. In spite of this betrayal, he continues his resistance activity far from the Strait. Wabnokwe acknowledges that she finds incomprehensible the struggles her former lover describes and that it is hard for her to distinguish his side from his adversary's. She attributes her difficulties to his use of unfamiliar vocabulary in the letters he writes to her.

The activities of the two daughters, Marti and Mendideti, during a brief stay on the Strait make Wabnokwe uneasy, even though, with them, there is no problem with vocabulary. Her evaluation of their activities comes at the end of Chapter Seven of Book Two of *The Strait*. Moník, a friend of Wabnokwe's from childhood, had married for money, intending to use the influence and wealth of the husband's family for good causes.

> Mendideti attached herself to Moník in a relationship that repelled Wabnokwe, a relationship that lacked the mutuality of friendship. Moník was enthralled by what she saw as a replica of her own youthful self and was ready to give her all to the young world-changer. Mendideti found Moník useful as a window to the wealth and poverty of the village, as a guide to the Strait's politics, but she showed only contempt toward Moník's wealth, house, views and greying hair. Mendideti interested herself in the trial of an escaped slave who had taken refuge on the Strait, and she sent Moník on errands to influential [local families] who might pressure the judges into releasing the refugee and initiating a trial against the southern pioneer who treated another human being as property. Wabnokwe shared Marti's enthusiasm for the outcome, but she did not share her daughter's admiration for Mendideti's ability to turn Moník into something that could be wielded like an instrument, like property.
>
> . . .
>
> The various meetings concerned with the trial of the fugitive had put Mendideti in contact with a circle of people Wabnokwe did not know, newcomers from the east who called themselves Abolitionists. Wabnokwe could not distinguish the Abolitionists from the other land-hungry pioneers who arrived in shiploads from the east, either in terms of their malice toward the original inhabitants of the land or in terms of their desire to denude the land of all its living beings. In Wabnokwe's experience, trader

Kin-sic had been a Slaver, trader Wit-nags an Abolitionist, and she dreaded the day when human prospects became narrowed to a choice between the spiritual descendants of those two men. Wabnokwe tried to reason with Marti, who at least listened to her, but she remembered her own one-time fanaticism in championing one of two identical armies, and she knew that Marti listened to her only out of politeness; she knew that Marti, like Mendideti, saw her as a meddlesome and ignorant old woman, at best a conservative know-nothing who could no longer grasp a great task, and at worst an accomplice of the slaveowning party. Mendideti avoided all contact with Wabnokwe.

Marti continued to attend the musicales, but Wabnokwe gradually woke up to the awareness that Marti was not there for the music, but as Mendideti's emissary. Marti was doing what Wabnokwe herself had done in an almost-forgotten past; she was using the salon gatherings as occasions for recruiting admiring young men to her and Mendideti's cause. Marti's first convert was haughty Fran Boms, who became as eloquent as Mendideti herself in voicing Mendideti's arguments against slavery. Marti's second convert was Benji-may who, although less than eloquent, formulated his lifelong hatred of slavery with his own words. Benji-may's unwillingness or inability to parrot the style and content of the party's leader made him an incomplete convert, and he complained to Wabnokwe that in Marti's eyes he remained a powerless and ignorant provincial, useless to the cause. This angered him, because his own hatred of slavery was fully as genuine as Mendideti's, whereas the complete convert, Fran Boms, merely pretended to feel the views he aired. According to Benji-may, Fran Boms was not interested in slavery but only in Marti, and the thing he liked most in Marti was her fanaticism; the elder Boms had once followed a similar fanatic who had become an emperor, and the son expected fanatical Marti to go far.

Benji-may told Wabnokwe that Mendideti and Marti had joined a secret club which styled itself an underground railroad, and that Mendideti had risen to prominence in this club by donating large quantities of Moník's money. Fran Boms was ready to join this club, but Benji-may despite his love for Marti, had misgivings. The ostensible aim of the club was to secure freedom for escaped slaves, an aim Benji-may approved. But the only concrete activities Benji-may had seen the club perform had consisted of coordination, administration, politics,

money, in short Business, the very activities his father Jay-may
had wanted Benji-may to take up, activities that had repelled
both of Jay-may's sons.

Wabnokwe reflects on her detachment from the activities of
Dehenyante and the daughters in 1832, ten years before her death.
She realizes that she is no longer at the center of Le Monde, but is
almost oblivious to the social and racial snobbery of Detroit society.
Her last decade is spent rescuing individual victims who, had her
youthful goal been realized, would have been part of a community
of all the Strait's residents, a community synthesizing two cultures.
She never loses her courage or renounces her principles although
she comes to see some of her youthful actions in a new light. She
respects Obenabi's integrity and revises her opinion about the
importance of his bundle. Calling the government's removal policies
"terrorizing the tamed," Wabnokwe, like Obenabi, refuses to leave
the Peninsula.

Woven into *The Strait* is a poignant commentary on the fortuitous
nature of one's life experiences: Obenabi, the rememberer of Rootkin
ways, never meets Dehenyante, the committed resister to Capital's
domestication. That their paths should not cross was carefully constructed. In a marginal note Fredy asks himself what their exchanges
and collaboration might have yielded.

In Fredy's attempt to answer the questions: How did human
society become the way it is? How can it be changed? he turned to
numerous other rememberers. His bibliography for *The Strait* lists
several hundred books. Some were relevant to a specific character
in the story. The four books at the top of the outline for Wabnokwe's
life are: James Joyce's *Ulysses,* Nikos Kazantzakis's *The Odyssey,*
Friedrich Nietzsche's *Thus Spake Zarathustra* and Henri Bergson's
The Two Sources of Morality and Religion.

Equating the world-changers with world-destroyers, Fredy's final
story leaves the reader with no explicit models. But it records
historically real social alternatives and it depicts honestly the situation encountered by the individual resister.

Fredy knew collective resistance would be needed to oppose the
ideological and technological violence of the modern world. His experiences in Paris in May 1968 gave him hope that creative insurgency
could cause the world of Capital to crumble. In those weeks he saw
the everyday routine overturned—completely and without warning.

He saw formerly docile order-takers carrying out self-defined projects; he saw authority ignored. In the years following May 1968, Fredy made efforts to initiate collective acts of resistance. He studied and analyzed successes and failures. Avoiding the word "revolutionary," he observed that to be "revolutionary" a project must culminate in revolution. He maintained that he had discovered no models which satisfied his requirements for "revolutionary."

The hopeful euphoria Fredy felt in 1968 dissipated during ensuing decades, and his eager wish to participate in a collective effort to abolish repressive social institutions went unrealized. His search for an appropriate agency for social change was also unsuccessful. He nevertheless remained committed to these goals both in his personal life and in intellectual projects. He examined, with sympathy and attention, attempts of a variety of resisters; and used his impulses for craftsmanship to produce attractive publications hoping, through them, to communicate with (in Sophia's words) "his likes." Consistent with his Sartrean psychology that one should view choices as exemplary, he shunned all institutional links and ignored media commodities (with occasional concessions to films and classical music).

In a number of ways Fredy's life resembled that of his professor from the 1950s, C. Wright Mills. Both were intellectuals ill at ease in the academy; both probed the mechanisms of modern society with a view to changing it; a failing heart brought both a premature death.

But in significant ways Fredy's intellectual trajectory differed from Mills'. In the last years of his life, Mills saw the Cuban Revolution as promising a new beginning. Full of hope that similar movements for liberation could emerge elsewhere, Mills recommended the Rocky Mountains to U.S. dissidents as an ideal refuge for insurgent guerrillas. Fredy put no hope in liberating armies, even indigenous ones, so the Rocky Mountains' defensive advantages had little appeal for him.

If, on occasion, Fredy termed himself a "recluse," he remained committed to human society – both in the abstract and to his many friends. He lived his life with gusto: music-making, eating, discussing, swimming; as well as contemplating, reading and writing. When we met, he was 22 years old. He already quoted approvingly a poem written in the seventeenth century by Andrew Marvell. One couplet seemed to have a particular relevance to him:

But at my back I always hear
Time's wingèd chariot hurrying near, . . .

Even then, Fredy sensed the chariot's approach and he accepted the poet's advice. With determination and high spirits—as well as a sense of urgency—Fredy ventured forth on his odyssey. I am not alone in feeling privileged to have shared part of the journey.

Lorraine Perlman
February 1989
Detroit

Bibliography

articles in *The Daily Bruin,* publication of The University of California at Los Angeles, Fall 1953(?) through January 1955.

articles in *The Observer,* Los Angeles, February - June 1955.

"The New Freedom": Corporate Capitalism, self-published in New York City, 1961 (91 copies).

Plunder, a play, self-published in New York City, 1962; Black & Red (Detroit), 1973.

"Cold War Mythology" (a review of *The Cold War and Its Origins, 1917-1970* by D.F. Fleming), *The Minority of One,* July 1962.

(with John Ricklefs) "Journey of a Pacifist, or The Birth of a Revolutionary Consciousness," 1962, unpublished.

(with John Ricklefs) "Man's Transformation of Nature," 1964, unpublished.

"The Structure of Backwardness," Master's thesis submitted to the University of Belgrade's Economics Faculty, 1965, unpublished.

* "Conditions for the Development of a Backward Region," Doctoral dissertation submitted to the University of Belgrade's Law Faculty, 1966, unpublished.

"Critical Education," *The Journal of General Education,* (Vol. 19, No. 3) October 1967, Pennsylvania State University Press.

"Corporate-Military Culture and the Social Sciences," 1967, mimeographed.

* "Essay on Commodity Fetishism," *Telos,* Buffalo, N.Y., Number 6, Fall 1970; later published as the introductory essay to I.I. Rubin's *Essay on Marx's Theory of Value,* Black & Red (Detroit), 1972; published as a 40-page pamphlet (which includes "The Fetish Speaks") by New England Free Press (Somerville, Mass.), 1975.

*This work has been translated.

"Ricardo and Preobrazhensky: Prophets of Two Systems," 1968, mimeographed.

"Corporate-Military Training or Education?" *Western Activist*, Kalamazoo, (no volume number) October 19, 1967.

"New Left Politics," *Western Activist*, Kalamazoo, (Vol. 3, No. 10) November 16, 1967.

"We, the Responsible," *Western Activist*, Kalamazoo, (Vol. 4, No. 3) January 25, 1968.

"Some Observations on the Vietnam War" (a lecture given on February 21, 1968), *Western Activist*, Kalamazoo, (Vol. 4, No. 8) February 29, 1968.

"The Second French Revolution: Chronology of Events," *Western Herald*, Kalamazoo, (Vol. 52, No. 91) June 14, 1968.

" 'Action Committees' Forge Alliances," *The Guardian*, New York City, (Vol. 20, No. 39) June 29, 1968.

"Liberated Censier," July-August 1968, unpublished.

"An Introduction to Marx," January 1969, unpublished.

"Anything Can Happen," *Black & Red No. 1*, Kalamazoo, September 1968.

(with L. Perlman) "Chicago: August, 1968," *Black & Red No. 2*, Kalamazoo, October 1968.

" 'Down With the Red Bourgeoisie' of Yugoslavia," *Black & Red No. 3*, Kalamazoo, November 1968.

(with B & R collaborators) "We Called a Strike and No One Came or Confessions of SDSers," *Black & Red No. 4*, Kalamazoo, Christmas 1968; published as a 48-page pamphlet by Black & Red (Detroit), 1973.

"The Fetish Speaks" (comics), *Black & Red No. 5*, Kalamazoo, January 1969.

(with B & R collaborators) "The University is a Provocation," *Black & Red No. 6*, Kalamazoo, March 22, 1969.

"I Accuse this Liberal University of Terror and Violence," *Black & Red No. 6*, Kalamazoo, March 22, 1969. Also published as a separate 12-page pamphlet in 1969.

"The Revolutionary Project," *Black & Red No. 6½*, Detroit, 1969.

(with Roger Gregoire) *Worker-Student Action Committees, France, May '68*, Black & Red (Kalamazoo), 1969; reprinted in Detroit in 1970.

* *The Reproduction of Daily Life*, Black & Red (Detroit), 1969, 1972; reprinted in Arthur Lothstein, ed., *"All We are Saying,"* Capricorn Books (New York), 1971; reprinted by Dark Star, Phoenix Press (London), 1989.

* *The Incoherence of the Intellectual: C. Wright Mills' Struggle to Unite Knowledge and Action*, Black & Red (Detroit), 1970.

(with L. Perlman) *Manual for Revolutionary Leaders* (attributed to Michael Velli), Black & Red (Detroit), 1972, 1974.

Letters of Insurgents (attributed to S. Nachalo & Y. Vochek), Black & Red (Detroit), 1976.

"Ten Theses on the Proliferation of Egocrats," *The Fifth Estate*, Detroit, (Vol. 12, No. 10) September 1977.

"Progress and Nuclear Power," *The Fifth Estate*, Detroit, (Vol. 14, No. 2) April 18, 1979.

* "Anti-Semitism and the Beirut Pogrom," *The Fifth Estate*, (Vol. 17, No. 3) Fall 1982; published as a 16-page pamphlet by Left Bank Books (Seattle), 1983.

"Against Leviathan," *The Fifth Estate*, Detroit, (Vol. 17, No. 4) Winter 1982-83.

Against His-story, Against Leviathan! Black & Red (Detroit), 1983.

* "The Continuing Appeal of Nationalism," *The Fifth Estate*, Detroit, (Vol. 19, No. 4) Winter 1984; published as a 58-page pamphlet by Black & Red (Detroit), 1985; published as a 32-page pamphlet by Dark Star, Phoenix Press (London), n.d. [1988].

"The Machine Against the Garden, Two Essays," *The Fifth Estate*, Detroit, (Vol. 20, No. 2) October 7, 1985.

The Strait (Vol. 1) *Book of Obenabi. His Songs*, Black & Red (Detroit), 1988.

The Strait (Vol. 2) "Book of Robert Dupré. His Tales," Incomplete and unpublished.

Translations of F. Perlman's Texts

Uslovi Razvoja Privredno Zaostalog Prodrucja s Posebnim Osvrtom na Kosovo i Metohiju, translation of doctoral dissertation, 1966. Mimeographed.

"La réproduction de la vie quotidienne," *L'Homme et la société*, Paris, No.15, 1970.

"Naissance d'un mouvement revolutionnaire en Yougoslavie," *L'Homme et la société*, Paris, No. 16, 1970.

Il feticismo delle merci, Lampugnani Nigri Editore (Milano), 1972.

"El fetichismo de la mercancia," in I.I. Rubin, *Ensayos sobre la teoria marxista del Valor*, Ediciones Pasado y Presente (Buenos Aires), 1974.

Vad Faan Haller vi pa med?! eller Reproduktionen av Vardagslivet, distributed by Socialism eller barbari (Stockholm), 1974.

A reprodução da vida quotidiana, Textos Exemplares (Lisbon), n.d. [1975].

L'incoherence de l'intellectuel (excerpts), Mimeographed, no publisher listed, 1977.

Antisemitisme et pogrome de Beyrouth, l'Insécurité Sociale (Paris), 1987.

"Antisemitismo e pogrom di Beirut," *Anarchismo,* Catania, No. 60, April 1988.

L'appel constant du nationalisme, l'Insécurité Sociale (Paris), 1986.
– –Edition Au bord de l'Arve, 1989.

"Il Costante Richiamo del nazionalismo," *Anarchismo,* Catania, No. 58, October 1987.

Works Translated by Fredy Perlman

(with Miloš Samardžija) I.I. Rubin, *Ocherki po teorii stoimosti marksa,* Gosudarstvennoe Isdatel'stvo (Moscow, Leningrad), 1928.

Mouvement du 22 mars, *Ce n'est qu'un début, continuons le combat,* presented by E. Copfermann, "Cahiers libres" 124, Maspero (Paris), 1968. Portions of the translation appeared in *Caw!* (SDS journal), New York City, Issue No. 3, Fall [1968].

(with five collaborators) Guy Debord, *Société du Spectacle,* Editions Buchet-Chastel (Paris), 1967. *Society of the Spectacle* was published by Black & Red (Detroit) in 1970 and a revised edition was printed in 1977.

Passages from Voline, *La révolution inconnue,* Editions Pierre Belfond (Paris), 1969. The passages in question, those omitted from the 1954-55 Freedom Press (London) edition, were included in the Black & Red (Detroit) edition of *The Unknown Revolution,* 1974.

(with L. Perlman) Peter Arshinov, *Istoriya Makhnovskogo Dvizhenija,* Berlin, 1923. *History of the Makhnovist Movement* was published by Black & Red (Detroit) in 1974.

Jacques Camatte, "Errance de l'humanité; Conscience represssive; Communisme," and "Declin du mode de production capitaliste ou declin de l'humanité?" *Invariance,* Brignoles, (Année VI, Série II, No. 3) 1973. The translation of the two essays, with the title *The Wandering of Humanity,* was published by Black & Red (Detroit) in 1975.

Texts about Fredy and his Works

David Porter, "Fredy Perlman: An Appreciation," *Kairos,* New York City, (Vol. 2, No. 1) 1986.

Reviews of *Against His-story, Against Leviathan!*

Paul Buhle, "Saint Alive!" in *Voice Literary Supplement,* New York City, No. 23, February 1984.
Jimmy Griffin in *RFD,* Bakersville, N.C., Summer 1985.
Jacques Depelchin, "For History, But Against His-story," *African Economic History,* 1988.

Appendix

"Letter to Dimitri"

Black Rose Books, Montreal

Dear Dimitri,

Thank you for your letter of November 19.

We would very much like to have a cordial relationship. I do not want to "cut off a relationship so ruthlessly on the basis of one stupid letter." But I want the nature of the relationship to be clear.

I'm sorry you were "shocked, hurt and saddened" by my previous letter, in which I responded to your letter of November 8 which we experienced as a direct slap in the face; I tried to explain why we were so shocked, hurt and saddened. I'm even more sorry that you understood my explanation as being so trivial that it prompted you to comment: ". . . it is strictly out of order to throw piety and self-righteousness at each other, as to who is poorer, who is more anti-capitalist and non-commercial."

I will try to be very clear about my understanding of the nature of our relationship.

You refer to your purchase of 500 (or 600) copies of Rubin's book as a precedent, a sort-of model, of "our relationship," and you refer to this transaction as a "common project," and thus as a basis for our present and future relations.

I think you should know that we did not regard our relation with you over the Rubin books as a "common project," but rather as something quite opposite from that. Your letter of November 8 made it clear to us that you were not only completely insensitive to the absolute one-sidedness of this relationship, but that, on the contrary, you were ready to make the very worst elements of that relationship a basis for present and future "collaboration" with us.

First of all, at the risk of boring you, I should try to make clear what I mean by a "common project," not in order to "throw piety and self-righteousness," but in order to explain why I will not agree to do what you want. Very concretely: our publication of Voline's and Arshinov's books are being done as common projects: Lorraine and I are working together with Ann Allen and Andy Tymowski (of Chicago Solidarity). The nature of our relationship is not at all abstract. All four of us were enthusiastic about the projects when we engaged ourselves in them. From the day we began, each one of the four has been concretely and personally engaged in every phase of the work. We not only edited and corrected the manuscripts together, and split the work involved in typesetting them; Ann and Andy came from Chicago to Detroit to learn photography, binding, and even helped us do some of the work necessary to maintain the print shop (not to mention that Andy had transported to Detroit the machine with which we will bind these books). I think I've given enough details: they speak for themselves; they lucidly describe the nature of the "common project."

Let me now describe, in detail, our experiences with you over Rubin's book, experiences which are for you the basis for "all our relationship and common projects":

a) On March 1, 1973, you ordered from us 50 copies of Rubin's book, and asked us about the possibility of sending you 300 *unbound* copies. We sent you the 50 copies *immediately*. A week later (on March 10) we asked you specific questions about the unbound copies, namely: "we need to know at what stage you would prefer to have them. If your binder is able to saw the signatures before putting the cover on, you would prefer. . . uncollated signatures. . . Or do you want the books collated, bound and trimmed?" (Eight months later you still hadn't answered this question; in contrast to all the work you had us do for you during those months, you did not even spend the time *to look at* a bound book. A standard hardback consists of signatures which are sewn to each other, and it can be made with our signatures before the spine is trimmed. The paperback, on the other hand, consists of loose sheets glued to the cover; these can no longer be sewn. It was only from your letter of Nov. 19th that we figured out that what you wanted was to pay the price for unbound books while at the same time having us collate, bind and trim them—because your "binder" doesn't make regular hard bound books at all; he apparently takes paperbacks, slices off the spine, leaving virtually no margin between the spine and the text, and slaps on "hard covers" over the loose sheets, emerging with a really cheap and half-assed binding job which is then sold expensively as a "bound hard-cover book.")

b) On March 14 you answered our question, with your characteristic "haste": "If we order the books in signatures, when can these be delivered? Immediately?" And on November 19th you still don't know which you want! "We would have preferred the printed book without the paper cover." What does that mean? Does it mean anything to you? Perhaps you meant to say that you wanted the *bound* book without the cover? But that doesn't mean anything either if the binding process consists of gluing loose pages to the cover: removing the cover removes the binding. (I'm restraining myself to the limit, Dimitri, even though I feel like exploding; what I really feel like asking is: Why the fuck do you act so ignorant about this for over eight months — is it because this is not a question for an Intellectual to deal with, but for a *manual* worker?)

c) In the same letter (March 14) you asked us to send you the books "in parcels of five. Separate the mailing of each parcel by a day or so. This will help us avoid customs duties."

[Please read carefully, Dimitri, because otherwise you will again fail to understand that our attitude has nothing to do with throwing piety, but with a refusal to be exploited by you again. Your "explanation" that your Nov. 8 letter was written in haste explains nothing; that same "haste" characterizes *all* your letters.]

d) On March 20, you asked for 100 more copies of Rubin's book, making a total of 150 — with the following list of instructions: mail in parcels of 5, separate each shipment by a day, mark each parcel "for educational . . .etc.," include a slip in each saying "not for re-sale." Did you (or do you) have any idea how much work that is? As if to "lessen our load" you added the following generous comment: "All this can be avoided if someone can drive over the border and mail them in Canada." (How and when did we acquire this heavy burden which you were so generously helping us avoid?) But at no time did *you* volunteer to drive over the border and lug the cartons across; *you gratuitously assumed* that Lorraine and I would do the packing and marking, or the lifting and carrying, or else it would not get done at all.

e) But we didn't take for granted a division of labor in which you give instructions and we do the work. Furthermore, I told you this *at that time*. You were not *unaware* of this; you *disregarded* it. In a letter I wrote on March 20 in response to your first instructions (of March 14th) I said: "We do not want to pack them in 11 pound parcels . . . It's too much work . . . We don't know anything about the customs duties." I erred in that letter: I should have been more explicit; I should have said, on March 20: "If you don't want to pay for the customs duties, and don't want to do anything at all except ask Lorraine and me to do a mound of extra work, then please don't ask us for the books."

In my March 20th letter I made one, single, modest request: "Could you pay for the books as soon as you get them? . . . we're in the process of buying an expensive binding machine . . ." I consider that this was an eminently fair request, since writing a check and mailing it was the extent to which you "participated" in the "common project." And wouldn't you know it! This was the one time you did not act hastily! We bought the binding machine, went broke, borrowed money from friends. *Three months later*—on June 26—I was placed in the position of having to write you a "bill-collecting" letter; this was intensely insulting to us *especially* because we had in the end talked ourselves into lugging the cartons to a Windsor post office.

f) You did not pay for these books until July 4th! At that time you asked for 500 more copies. On this occasion you asked us to transform the format of the book—in fact, to wipe out every trace suggesting that we had worked on the book. Put Black Rose Books, Montreal, on the cover, the spine, the back cover, the title page, and even: "There is a problem with the printing co-op bug's mention . . . is there a way of not mentioning Detroit?" In other words: Rubin's book is published and printed by Black Rose Books, Montreal. This was a standard *capitalist* relationship, exactly as described in the top paragraph of p. 21 of M. Velli's *Manual*. Of course there were reasons. There always are.

It was *our mistake* to agree to have anything to do with this type of relationship. We were impelled by very ordinary motives: we were absolutely broke, and desperately needed the money to pay debts acquired from the purchase of the binder. And you took advantage of our situation to the limit, all the way to stating flatly that, after doing all that work wiping out all traces of our work on the book: "The books must be mailed in Canada"!

All of which we did! And once again, although you paid for more than half the books soon after you received them, you did not hasten to send us a balance of $283 which we needed, and once again I had to write "bill collecting" letters, once on September 9th, and once again two months later, on November 2!

What I have described is an altogether one-sided relationship: it is a "division of tasks" in which you spend a few minutes writing hasty instructions, while we spend portions of our lives satisfying them. You have very good reasons for wanting to continue this type of relationship. We don't.

I want to be very clear: we will never again voluntarily agree to saddle ourselves with a relationship that resembles the one described above, and we consider it malicious to refer to such a relationship as a "common project."

As for cordial relations: by all means, let's have cordial and equitable relations, relations which contain at least a *trace* of mutual respect for each other's time and labor!

Neither in the present letter, nor in my November 15th letter, do I want to put an end to cordial and equitable relations. On the contrary, I would like to *begin* to have such relations with you.

You at no time expressed any desire in engaging in a "common project" with us by doing the actual work of the project, even to the extent of picking up boxes in Vermont or New York and lugging them across the border yourself. So it's not a question of a common project. You merely want to purchase a number of books. Fine. As soon as Arshinov's book is printed, we'll send you one or more copies, and we'll tell you the cost for bulk orders. You can then order as many as you want. We will send them to you *after* we receive full payment for the books in advance. We will not lug the cartons anywhere; we will have them picked up at the Printing Co-op by Railway Express (or any shipping company you suggest, provided they pick them up at the print shop). If the customs duties will be too high for you, we will ship them wherever you suggest in the US, and you can transport them across the border. If you don't want them shipped from Detroit to Montreal, and don't want them shipped from Detroit to some other place, then please don't order them. If you are genuinely concerned to help Arshinov's book reach Canadian readers and libraries, by all means advertise it! (Voline's book as well.) We will be glad to send copies to any and all Canadian readers and libraries who request them, and there will be no problem with customs duties.

I am writing on my own account only, and am not speaking for all the people engaged in the project of publishing Arshinov's and Voline's books. I am sending a copy of this letter to the comrades in Chicago who are sharing the work with us; if they have additional, or different, responses to your suggestions, I am sure they will write to you directly.

Best wishes,

Fredy

Fredy's Early Notes on the World-Changers

Nov. 77

*First sketch of the project
of Sabina & Intellicus*

the task is not to interpret, etc....

all right. then let's take the world-changers: Intellicus & Sabina. the positive and its negative, the dominant social praxis & its dialectical inversion, & let's "interpret" what the task of changing the world changed it to. Define them as:

Intellicus, illustrious magnus, booster — scientific practice, practical science, namely *praxis*, world-changing, Production, Capital — runaway

Sabina, "the mirror of Production," Capital's daughter: craftsman, worker, proletarian; the rebel is heir, the "workers' movement" — negation is "uberlebung" — until the breakdown, when she rediscovers a more fundamental resistance at her origins.

But let's not interpret the world-changers, limiting interpretation to the ascertainment of the fact that their epoch is over. let's, rather, celebrate them, telling and singing of their great deeds, giving their epoch its epic. as for changing the world, let's embellish it with a song, by singing at its funeral.

Nov 77

Rudiments of procedure

The mythologization of Selina & Satellicus is carried out by Selina between 1965 and 1968 — it is her "final oration" to her friends and disciples.

Selina tries to discover her destination by recapitulating her own trajectory — and as soon as she begins, she realizes she has to trace Satellicus's, because hers is nothing but the negative of his.

thus her opus consists of 2 works (each multi-volumes): an autobiography, and a biography of Satellicus. She kept two sets of notes & diagrams, intending the separation to reflect two poles, opposites — but already before 1968 she knows that one is the shadow of the other.

Her procedure with <u>Satellicus</u> is to narrate history as biography, & mythologize history, accepting the facts of Albert's' life only as hooks on which to hang symbols. The correspondence between the myth & the man can be evaluated through independent accounts by Luisa, perhaps by survivors & doctors who knew him, & by Tina's research.

Her procedure with herself (as yet vague — it's '65) is to celebrate the "seed" Satellicus planted in her — thus it is personal, history entering thru ref to him — until the hurried re-write of 1968, when she sees the essential unity of the opposites because both of their epochs have simultaneously come to an end.

nov 77

a note on the research, outlining & writing

the song sings of the rise & fall of capital & labor, or perhaps even of the decline of civilization — & sings of it in the epic spirit of Greek storytellers narrating the decline of the earth goddesses.

If the song is worthy, then it doesn't need artifices to make it so. So time & energy need not then be spent on plots, denouements, character developments, nor even themes, since all of these are organic components of the subject being sung. Instead, the energy should be devoted to compilation and to digging & probing, so as to discover & bring to light the depths of the subject itself.

Some of these "depths" are in the correspondences between macrocosm & microcosm — & they are thus to be found only through the developments of the sequences - esp the historical ones.

(Selina eventually becomes aware of the similarity to a medieval procedure — but this should be no surprise, since the story is also a recapitulation from the vantage point of its origin)

note that _he_ is Capital, whereas _she_ is humanity, worker, child, and _woman_

Nov 72

to start

1. Keep these notes consecutively numbered, regardless of subject, to avoid the confusion of partitions (at least until the discovery of a more useful method). Keep track of notes on key sheets.

2. Enter the main "real events" for Salina & Satellicus on keys — for rudimentary frame of reference. Also some of the known personages: ~~Wilkins~~ (oops - yet to be developed)
   (Luise, Zebran & the Matthews go on Satellicus's key, even though they may not appear in Salina's narrative)
   (this means the Satellicus of her narrative may need another key, based on the first but mythologized) (all the first "Alberts")
   (Alberts in WWII - see notable biography of left nuclear physicist (or necromancer))
   In Salina's key, include Tissie, ~~Matthew~~ — prominently
   — Ron, Joe, Sophia — not so prominently —
   — her "friends and disciples" are yet to be created.

3. Historical notes should take precedence as soon as possible
   — each note's page # being recorded on the historical key
   from these notes should be elaborated correspondences with biographical events & characters

4. For the sake of a continual viability of the "environment," more general key charts can be constructed depicting the technology, population, ~~the~~ production, etc.

5. A major effort should be exerted to find <u>visual correspondences</u>.

PHOTO CREDITS

Frontispiece, Millard Berry
The photographers responsible for photos 1, 2 and 5 are unknown.
3. L. Perlman
4 Marty McReynolds
4. Marty McReynolds
6. using timer device on our Russian camera.
7. Roger Gregoire
8. L. Perlman
9. Carl Smith
10. Carl Smith
11. David Levison
12. K.D. Wolff
13. Jim O'Brien[?]
14. Maurice Fhima
15. L. Perlman
16. Frank Jackson

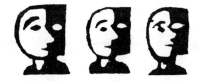